Study Guid

Managing Human Resources
Thirteenth Edition

George Bohlander
Arizona State University

Scott Snell
Cornell University

Prepared by

Thomas W. Lloyd
Westmoreland County Community College

THOMSON

SOUTH-WESTERN

Australia · Canada · Mexico · Singapore · Spain · United Kingdom · United States

THOMSON

SOUTH-WESTERN

Study Guide to accompany Managing Human Resources, 13e

George Bohlander, Scott Snell
Prepared by Thomas W. Lloyd

VP/Editorial Director:
Jack W. Calhoun

VP/Editor-in-Chief:
Mike Roche

Acquisitions Editor:
Joe Sabatino

Senior Developmental Editor:
Alice C. Denny

Marketing Manager:
Rob Bloom

Production Editor:
Heather Mann

Manufacturing Coordinator:
Diane Lohman

Media Developmental Editor:
Kristen Meere

Media Production Editor:
Karen Schaffer

Design Project Manager:
Rik Moore

Cover Designer:
Paul Neff

Cover Image:
© Diana Ong/Superstock

Printer:
Globus Printing, Inc.
Minster, OH

For permission to use material from this
text or product, contact us by
Tel (800) 730-2214
Fax (800) 730-2215
http://www.thomsonrights.com

For more information
contact South-Western,
5191 Natorp Boulevard,
Mason, Ohio, 45040.
Or you can visit our Internet site at:
http://www.swlearning.com

PREFACE

The student Study Guide that companies the 13th Edition of *Managing Human Resources* by Bohlander & Snell offers something new and exciting to motivate your learning in this course. The objective of the student Study Guide is to increase your understanding human resources management theory and concepts.

Learning Objectives. After you have read the chapter in the text, read the Learning Objectives to review what you should have learned from the chapter.

Chapter Summary. The Chapter Summary is prepared in conjunction with the learning objectives. Read and study the Chapter Summary carefully. Review any concepts in the text that you did not completely understand.

Self-Test Questions. The Self-Test section includes three separate self-test exercises – **Multiple Choice** questions, **True/False** questions, and a **Definition Review** in the form of matching questions. Test questions are new and revised. **Real-life Application** questions have been added to improve your understanding of business as it relates to theoretical concepts. Finally, a **How to** section has been added to the 13th Edition to improve your understanding of Human Resources function as it applies to recruitment, selection, orientation and training, and a focus on continuous improvement through the creation of workforce diversity.

When reading and studying the textbook, use the opportunity to apply and integrate the knowledge you have gained to answer the questions that appear in this Study Guide.

Answers. The answers to all the Multiple Choice, True/False, Definition Review, Applications, and How to questions are found at the end of each chapter. Check your answers only after you have answered all of the questions. Reviewing any incorrect answers may suggest the need for further review of the text material. You can easily find the material in the textbook by using the learning objective icon that appears with each Multiple Choice, True/False, and Application question.

Have a good semester.

MANAGING HUMAN RESOURCES, 13e, by Bohlander and Snell

Table of Contents

CHAPTER 1

THE CHALLENGE OF HUMAN RESOURCES MANAGEMENT

You will be able to learn how firms gain sustainable competitive advantage with and through people. You will be able to comprehend the concept of globalization and the impact it has created on human resources management. This awareness will provide a perspective with which to interpret current practices, problems, and issues more clearly. This chapter is designed to make you aware of the challenges of human resources management that you will encounter in the work environment. In reading this chapter you will be able to understand how information technology challenges managers and employees. This chapter will also acquaint you with the growing body of knowledge being accumulated within the field. In this chapter you will learn the importance of change management and the following tools that are utilized by human resources managers, such as, the development of intellectual capital and how total quality management and reengineering challenge human resources systems. Finally, you will be able to learn the roles and competencies that challenge human resources management. You will be able to understand the impact of cost pressures on human resources policies and changing demographics and employee concerns pertaining to human resources management.

LEARNING OBJECTIVES

After studying this chapter you should be able to

 Identify how firms gain sustainable competitive advantage through people.

 Explain how globalization is influencing human resources management.

 Describe the impact of information technology on managing people.

 Identify the importance of change management.

 State human resources' role in developing intellectual capital.

Differentiate how total quality management and reengineering influence human resources systems.

 Discuss the impact of cost pressures on human resources policies.

 Discuss the primary demographic and employee concerns pertaining to human resources management.

 Provide examples of the roles and competencies of today's human resources managers.

CHAPTER SUMMARY RELATING TO LEARNING OBJECTIVES

People have always been central to organizations, but their strategic importance is growing in today's knowledge-based industries. An organization's success increasingly depends on the knowledge, skills, and abilities of employees, particularly as they help establish a set of core competencies that distinguish an organization from its competitors. When employees' talents are valuable, rare, difficult to imitate, and organized, an organization can achieve a sustained competitive advantage through people.

Globalization influences approximately 70 to 85 percent of the U.S. economy and affects the free flow of trade among countries. This influences the number and kinds of jobs that are available and requires that organizations balance a complicated set of issues related to managing people in different geographies, cultures, legal environments, and business conditions. Human resources functions such as staffing, training, compensation, and the like have to be adjusted to take into account the differences in global management.

Advanced technology has tended to reduce the number of jobs that require little skill and to increase the number of jobs that require considerable skill, a shift we refer to as moving from "touch labor" to knowledge work. This displaces some employees and requires that others be retrained. In addition, information technology has influenced human resources management through human resources information systems (HRIS) that streamline the processing of data and make employee information more readily available to managers.

4   Both proactive and reactive change initiatives require human resources managers to work with line managers and executives to create a vision for the future, establish an architecture that enables change, and communicate with employees about the processes of change.

5   In order to "compete through people" organizations have to do a good job of managing human capital: the knowledge, skills, and capabilities that have value to organizations. Managers must develop strategies for identifying, recruiting, and hiring the best talent available; developing these employees in ways that are firm-specific; helping them to generate new ideas and generalize them through the company; encouraging information sharing; and rewarding collaboration and teamwork.

6   In order to respond to customer needs better, faster, and more cheaply, organizations have instituted total-quality management (TQM) and reengineering programs. Each of these programs requires that human resources be involved in changing work processes, training, job design, compensation, and the like. Human resources issues also arise when communicating with employees about the new work systems, just as with any change initiative.

7   In order to contain costs, organizations have been downsizing, outsourcing, leasing employees, and enhancing productivity. Human resources' role is to maintain the relationship between a company and its employees, while implementing the changes.

8   The workforce is becoming increasingly diverse and organizations are doing more to address employees concerns and to maximize the benefit of different kinds of employees. Demographic changes, social and cultural differences and changing attitudes toward work can provide a rich source of variety for organizations. But to benefit from diversity, managers need to recognize the potential concerns of employees and make certain that the exchange between the organization and employees is mutually beneficial.

9   In working with line managers to address the organization's challenges, human resources managers play a number of important roles; they are called on for advice and counsel, for various service activities, for policy formulation and implementation, and for employee advocacy. To perform these roles effectively, human resources managers must contribute business competencies, state-of-the-art human resources competencies, and change-management competencies. Ultimately, managing people is rarely the exclusive responsibility of the human resources function. Every manager's job is managing people, and successful companies are those that combine the expertise of human resources specialists with the experience of line managers to develop and utilize the talents of employees to their greatest potential.

REVIEW QUESTIONS

Multiple Choice

Choose the letter of the word or phrase that best completes each statement.

1. The key to a firm's success is based on establishing a set of
   a. human resources certification.
   b. human resources procedures on outsourcing.
   c. core competencies.
   d. all of the above.

2. The following criteria highlight the importance of people and show the closeness of human resources management to strategic management, **EXCEPT FOR**
   a. certification of people resources.
   b. resources are valued.
   c. resources must be rare.
   d. resources must be difficult to imitate.

3. The employee's skills, knowledge, and abilities are among the most distinctive investment of resources a company can develop. This process is known as
   a. employee leasing.
   b. position descriptions.
   c. employee empowerment.
   d. strategic management.

4. To compete in the 21st century, the focus of human resources management will be on the need to
   a. develop a production plan.
   b. rationalize scientific management principles.
   c. utilize organization development.
   d. develop a skilled and flexible workforce.

5. Efforts to lower trade barriers and open global markets to free flow of goods, services, and capital among nations have lead to trade zones called
   a. North American Free Trade Agreement (NAFTA).
   b. European Unification (EU).
   c. Asia Pacific Economic Cooperation (APEC).
   d. all of the above.

6. The North American Free Trade Agreement may soon be
   replaced by a broader set of economic agreements called the
   a. Free Trade Area of the Americas (FTAA).
   b. European Unification (EU).
   c. Asia Pacific Economic Cooperation (APEC).
   d. General Agreement on Tariffs and Trade (GATT).

7. When managers talk about "going global," they have to balance a
   complicated set of issues related to
   a. different geographies.
   b. different cultures.
   c. different laws and practices.
   d. all of the above.

8. The process where unlimited amounts of data can be stored,
   retrieved, and used in a wide variety of ways, from simple record
   keeping to controlling complex equipment is
   a. total quality management.
   b. telecommuting.
   c. reengineering of work.
   d. computer networks.

9. The concept that has changed the face of human resources
   management in the United States and abroad is known as
   a. information technology.
   b. employee empowerment.
   c. organization downsizing.
   d. employee leasing.

10. The basic ways information technology affects human resources
    would include the following **EXCEPT FOR**
    a. operational impact.
    b. relational impact.
    c. procedural impact
    d. transformational impact.

11. In order to be more successful organizations need to include the
    following **EXCEPT FOR**
    a. continuous improvement.
    b. outsourcing.
    c. reengineering.
    d. unionized plans.

4 _____ 12. The change initiated to take advantage of targeted opportunities, particularly in fast-changing industries where followers are not successful is
   a. proactive management.
   b. strategic organization.
   c. employee downsizing.
   d. human resource information system.

4 _____ 13. Major reasons why change efforts can fail due to human resources issues include the following **EXCEPT FOR**
   a. not creating a powerful coalition to guide the effort.
   b. lacking leaders who have vision.
   c. declaring victory too soon.
   d. establishing a sense of urgency.

5 _____ 14. The asset that describes the economic value of knowledge, skills, and capabilities is known as
   a. human capital.
   b. information technology.
   c. total-quality management.
   d. human resource information systems.

5 _____ 15. Human capital is intangible and elusive and cannot be managed the way organizations manage
   a. jobs.
   b. products.
   c. technologies.
   d. all of the above

6 _____ 16. A set of principles and practices whose core ideas include understanding customer needs, doing things right the first time, and striving for continuous improvement is
   a. reengineering of work.
   b. total-quality management.
   c. outsourcing.
   d. global management.

6 _____ 17. A statistical method of translating a customer's needs into separate tasks and defining the best way to perform each task is
   a. reengineering.
   b. Six Sigma.
   c. Total Quality Management.
   d. Human Resource Planning.

objective 6

_____ 18. The procedure, which describes "the fundamental rethinking and radical redesign of business processes to achieve dramatic improvements in cost, quality, service, and speed", is
a. human resource information.
b. total quality management.
c. reengineering.
d. international business.

objective 7

_____ 19. A process where an organization can essentially maintain its working relationships but shift the administrative costs of health care, retirement, and other benefits to the professional employer organization is
a. employee leasing.
b. employee turnover.
c. reengineering.
d. total quality management.

objective 7

_____ 20. The output gained from a fixed amount of inputs that organizations can increase, by either reducing the inputs or by increasing the amount that employees produce is known as
a. total quality management.
b. organization downsizing.
c. intellectual capital.
d. productivity.

objective 8

_____ 21. Employee productivity is the result of a combination of the following **EXCEPT FOR**
a. job dissatisfaction.
b. employee abilities.
c. motivation.
d. work environment.

objective 8

_____ 22. Women are fairly well represented in fast-growing occupations such as
a. health services.
b. construction.
c. accounting.
d. production.

objective 9

_____ 23. The major activities for which a human resources manager is typically responsible include the following, **EXCEPT FOR**
a. direct line managers.
b. service, advice, and counsel.
c. policy formulation and implementation.
d. employee advocacy.

(9)   24. Employers can encounter costly collective bargaining proposals,
                    threats of strike, and charges of unfair labor practices where
                    employees are organized into
                    a. self-managed teams.
                    b. labor unions.
                    c. quality circles.
                    d. lay advisory work groups.

(9)   25. As human resources managers assume a broader role in overall
                    organizational strategy, many of these managers will need to
                    acquire a complementary set of competencies such as
                    a. business mastery.
                    b. personal credibility.
                    c. change mastery.
                    d. all of the above.

True/False

Identify the following statements as True or False.

(1)   1. Experts now argue that the key to a firm's success is based on
                    establishing a set of core competencies.

(1)   2. To compete in the twenty-first century there is a need to recruit
                    and select a work force that is rigid and non-flexible in their work
                    skills.

(2)   3. From a human resources management perspective, globalization
                    is of interest only to large firms.

(2)   4. The globalization process impacts human resources management
                    through the recruitment of expatriate managers.

(3)   5. The introduction of advanced technology into an organization
                    tends to increase the number of jobs that require little skill and to
                    reduce the number of jobs that require considerable skill.

(3)   6. The most central use of technology in human resources
                    management is an organization's human resource information
                    system (HRIS).

3

_____ 7. Operational impact of information technology on human resources automates routine activities, alleviates the administrative burden, reduces costs, and improves productivity internal to the human resources function itself.

4

_____ 8. In managing change through human resources applications, people often welcome change because it requires them to modify or abandon ways of working that have been successful or at least familiar to them.

4

_____ 9. According to Dr. Marilyn Buckner, "Non-technical, unattended human factors are, in fact, most often the problem in failed change projects.

5

_____ 10. The value of human capital is intangible and cannot be managed the way organizations manage jobs, products, and technologies.

5

_____ 11. Staffing programs focus on identifying, recruiting, and hiring the minimum talent available.

5

_____ 12. Skill-based pay rewards employees for each new class of jobs they are capable of performing.

6

_____ 13. A systematic approach to reorientation and competitive strategies is Six Sigma.

6

_____ 14. Six Sigma's focus on continuous improvement drives the system towards equilibrium of supply exceeding demand.

6

_____ 15. Reengineering often requires that managers start over from scratch in rethinking how work should be done, how technology and people should interact, and how entire organizations should be structured.

7

_____ 16. Investments in reengineering, total quality management, human capital, technology, globalization, and the like are not very important for organizational competitiveness.

7

_____ 17. In terms of cost containment, labor costs are one of the lowest expenditures of any organization, particularly in service and knowledge-intensive companies.

7

_____ 18. Outsourcing simply means hiring someone outside the company to perform tasks that could be done internally.

8

_____ 19. Demographic changes in the workforce are changes in employee background, age, gender, and education levels.

_____ 20. To accommodate the shift in demographics, many organizations have decreased their efforts to recruit and train a more diverse workforce.

_____ 21. The attitudes, beliefs, values, and customs of people in a society are an integral part of their culture.

_____ 22. Employees today are more likely to define their personal success only in terms of financial gains.

_____ 23. Though most people still enjoy work and want to excel at it, they tend to be focused on finding routine, repetitive work and may pursue multiple careers rather than being satisfied with just "having a job."

_____ 24. Human resources managers are not exclusively responsible for coordinating programs and policies pertaining to people-related issues.

_____ 25. One of the enduring roles of human resources managers is to serve as an employee advocate—listening to the employees' concerns and representing their needs to be managers.

Matching

Match each term with the proper definition.

Terms

a. core competencies
b. downsizing
c. employee leasing
d. globalization
e. human capital
f. human resources information system HRIS

g. knowledge workers
h. managing diversity
i. outsourcing
j. proactive change
k. reactive change
l. reengineering
m. total-quality management (total quality management)

Definitions

_____ 1. employees whose responsibilities are expanded to include a richer array of activities such as planning, decision-making, and problem solving

_____ 2. when external forces affect an organization's performance and are seldom planned

_____ 3. represents the knowledge, skills, and capabilities of individuals that have economic value to an organization

_____ 4. set of principles and practices whose core ideas include understanding customer needs, doing things right the first time, and striving for continuous improvement

_____ 5. hiring someone outside the company to perform tasks that could be done internally

_____ 6. integrated knowledge sets within an organization that distinguishes it from its competitors and deliver value to customers

_____ 7. being aware of characteristics common to employees, while managing employees as individuals

_____ 8. trend toward opening up foreign markets to international trade and investment

_____ 9. change initiated by managers to take advantage of targeted opportunities, particularly in-fast changing industries where followers are not successful

_____ 10. the planned elimination of jobs within the organization

_____ 11. provides current and accurate data for purposes of control and decision making

_____ 12. an organization can essentially maintain its working relationships with employees but shift the administrative costs of health care, retirement, and other benefits to the vendor

_____ 13. the fundamental rethinking and radical redesign of business processes to achieve dramatic improvements in cost, quality, service, and speed

Applications

1 _____ 1. Disney, Southwest Airlines, and Mirage Resorts have developed a competitive advantage by creating unique cultures that get the most from employees through teamwork and
   a. are difficult to imitate.
   b. use labor unions.
   c. are strictly domestic operations.
   d. use outsourcing.

2 _____ 2. By partnering with firms in other regions of the world and using information technologies to coordinate distant parts of their businesses, companies such as Motorola, General Electric, and Toyota have shown that their vision for the future is to offer customers "anything, anytime, anywhere" around the world. This concept is known as
   a. domestic operation.
   b. globalization.
   c. scientific management.
   d. the Hawthorne studies.

7 _____ 3. Continental Airlines, Dial Corporation, and L.L. Bean have undertaken cost-cutting decisions to eliminate jobs. This process is known as
   a. budgetary analysis.
   b. behavioral science.
   c. human relations movement.
   d. downsizing.

8 _____ 4. Pacific Gas and Electric is making positive efforts to attract older workers, especially those who have taken
   a. vacation.
   b. career changes.
   c. early retirement.
   d. ergonomics retraining.

8 _____ 5. At Aetna Life, a 50 percent decrease in employee turnover has been achieved by offering
   a. tax incentives to small businesses.
   b. behavioral science programs.
   c. courses in scientific management principles.
   d. six-month parental leaves.

How to Develop A Working Knowledge

In developing a working knowledge one should concentrate on building a multi-skilled approach to prepare oneself for the job market. By a multi-skilled approach, it is important to have improved communication skills, computer skills, and decision and problem solving skills.

An individual's working knowledge should be integrated to the core competencies of the organization. The core competencies should be apart of the orientation and training one receives in joining an organization. These competencies should develop a competitive edge for the firm, whereby a customer-driven approach should be emphasized.

The cultural values of the organization should be understood and adhered to by everyone in the firm. The philosophy of management or the management styles that separate one organization from another should be understood. Each organization has its own management style, it is important to recognize this and adapt to it. For a career to be built on success one should be on a career tract to advance in the organization hierarchy. Growth opportunities should be recognized to perpetuate career opportunities when then become available.

SOLUTIONS

Multiple Choice:	**True/False:**	**Matching:**
1. c	1. True	1. g
2. a	2. False	2. k
3. d	3. False	3. e
4. d	4. True	4. m
5. d	5. False	5. i
6. a	6. True	6. a
7. d	7. True	7. h
8. d	8. False	8. d
9. a	9. True	9. j
10. c	10. True	10. b
11. d	11. False	11. f
12. a	12. True	12. c
13. d	13. False	13. l
14. a	14. False	
15. d	15. True	
16. b	16. False	
17. b	17. True	
18. c	18. True	
19. a	19. True	
20. d	20. False	
21. a	21. True	
22. a	22. False	
23. a	23. False	
24. b	24. True	
25. d	25. True	

False Statements from True/False

2. To compete in the twenty-first century there is a need to recruit and select a work force that is **flexible** in their work skills.

3. From a human resources management perspective, globalization is **not just something** of interest to large firms.

5. The introduction of advanced technology into an organization tends to **reduce** the number of jobs that require little skill and to **increase** the number of jobs that require considerable skill.

8. In managing change through human resources applications, people often **resist** change because it requires them to modify or abandon ways of working that have been successful or at least familiar to them.

11. Staffing programs focus on identifying, recruiting, and hiring the **best and brightest** talent available.

13. A systematic approach to **quality** and competitive strategies is Six Sigma.

14. Six Sigma's focus on continuous improvement drives the system towards **disequilibrium** of supply exceeding demand.
16. Investments in reengineering, total quality management, human capital, technology, globalization, and the like **are very important** for organizational competitiveness.
20. To accommodate the shift in demographics, many organizations have **increased** their efforts to recruit and train a more diverse workforce.
22. Employees today are **less** likely to define their personal success only in terms of financial gains.
23. Though most people still enjoy work and want to excel at it, they tend to be focused on finding **interesting** work and may pursue multiple careers rather than being satisfied with just "having a job."

Applications:

1. a
2. b
3. d
4. c
5. d

CHAPTER 2

EQUAL EMPLOYMENT OPPORTUNITY
AND HUMAN RESOURCES MANAGEMENT

In this chapter you will learn how managers must be constantly aware of the laws and regulations governing the employment relationship. This is true for both federal and state regulations. Many of these laws concern the fair and equal employment of protected classes of workers, although equal employment opportunity (EEO) laws pertain to all members of the labor force. You will understand from this chapter that equal employment opportunity laws cover all aspects of employment, including recruitment, selection, training, promotion, and compensation. In hiring or supervision employees, you will know to give careful attention to the application of equal employment opportunity laws and regulations to prevent charges of discrimination. Finally, you will be able to distinguish how protected classes can sustain a charge of adverse impact, how an employer can establish a defense of adverse impact, and how the employer should establish an affirmative action program.

LEARNING OBJECTIVES

After studying this chapter you should be able to

 Explain the reasons behind the passage of equal employment opportunity legislation.

 Prepare an outline describing the major laws affecting equal employment opportunity. Describe bona fide occupational qualification and religious preference as equal employment opportunity issues.

 Discuss sexual harassment and immigration reform and control as equal employment opportunity concerns.

 Explain the use of the *Uniform Guidelines on Employee Selection Procedures*.

Provide examples illustrating the concept of adverse impact and apply the four-fifths rule.

 Discuss significant court cases impacting equal employment opportunity.

 Illustrate various enforcement procedures affecting equal employment opportunity.

 Describe affirmative action and the basic steps in developing an affirmative action program.

CHAPTER SUMMARY RELATING TO LEARNING OBJECTIVES

 Employment discrimination against blacks, Hispanics, women, and other groups has long been practiced by U.S. employers. Prejudice against minority groups is a major cause in their lack of employment gains. Government reports show that the wages and job opportunities of minorities typically lag behind those for whites. Factors that have influenced the growth of equal employment opportunity legislation: changing attitudes toward employment discrimination, published reports highlighting the economic problems of women, minorities, and older workers, and a growing body of disparate laws and government regulations covering discrimination.

Some of the significant laws that have been passed barring employment discrimination are:
- The Equal Pay Act of 1963 outlaws discrimination in pay, employee benefits, and pensions based on the worker's gender.
- Title VII of the Civil Rights Act of 1964 is the broadest and most significant of the antidiscrimination statues. The act bars discrimination in all human resources activities, including hiring, training, promotion, pay, employee benefits, and other conditions of employment. Discrimination is prohibited on the basis of race, color, religion, sex, or national origin.
- Age Discrimination in Employment Act of 1967 prohibits private and public employers from discriminating against persons 40 years of age or older in any area of employment because of age; exceptions are permitted where age is a bona fide occupational qualification.
- Equal Employment Opportunity Act of 1972, amended Title VII of Civil Rights Act of 1964, it strengthens Equal Employment Opportunity Commission's enforcement powers and extends coverage of Title VII to government employees, employees in higher education, and other employers and employees.

- The Pregnancy Discrimination Act of 1978 broadens the definition of sex discrimination to include pregnancy, childbirth, or related medical conditions; prohibits employers from discriminating against pregnant women in employment benefits if they are capable of performing their job duties.
- The Americans with Disabilities Act of 1990 prohibits discrimination in employment against persons with physical or mental disabilities or the chronically ill; enjoins employers to make reasonable accommodation to the employment needs of the disabled; covers employers with fifteen or more employees.
- The Civil Rights Act of 1991 provides for compensatory and punitive damages and jury trials in cases involving intentional discrimination; requires employers to demonstrate that job practices are job-related and consistent with business necessity; extends coverage to United States citizens working for American companies overseas.
- Uniformed Services Employment and Reemployment Rights Act of 1994 protects the employment rights of individuals who enter the military for short periods of service.
- A bona fide occupational qualification (BFOQ) permits discrimination where employer-hiring preferences are a reasonable necessity for the normal operation of the business. Freedom to exercise religious choice is guaranteed under the U.S. constitution. Title VII of the Civil Rights Act also prohibits discrimination based on religion in employment decisions, though it permits employer exemptions. The act defines religion to "include all aspects of religious observance and practice, as well as belief."

Sexual harassment and immigration reform and control are two areas of particular importance to managers. Extensive efforts should be made by all organizations to ensure that employees are free from all forms of sexually harassing conduct. Illegal immigration has adversely affected welfare services and educational and Social Security benefits. In 1986 Congress passed the Immigration Reform and Control Act. The act was passed to control unauthorized immigration by making it unlawful for a person or organization to hire, recruit, or refer for a fee, persons not legally eligible for employment in the United States. Employers must comply with the law by verifying and maintaining records on the legal rights of applicants to work in the United States.

The *Uniform Guidelines on Employment Selection Procedures* is designed to assist employers in complying with federal prohibitions against employment practices that discriminate on the basis of race, color, religion, gender, or national origin. The *Uniform Guidelines* provides employers with a framework for making legally enforceable decisions. Employers must be able to show that selection procedures are valid in predicting job performance.

5 Adverse impact plays an important role in proving employment discrimination. Adverse impact means that an employer's employment practices result in the rejection of a significantly higher percentage of members of minority and other protected groups for some employment activity. The four-fifths rule is a guideline to determine whether employment discrimination might exist. Disparate treatment is a situation in which protected class members receive unequal treatment or are evaluated by different standards.

6 The United States court system continually interprets employment law, and managers must formulate organizational policy in response to court decisions. Violations of the law will invite discrimination charges from protected groups or self-initiated investigation from government agencies. *Griggs v Duke Power, Albermarle Paper Company v Moody*, and *Wards Cove Packing Co. v Antonio* provided added importance to the *Uniform Guidelines. Meritor Savings Bank v Vinson, Harris v Forklift Systems Inc.*, and *TWA v Hardison* are instructive in the areas of sexual harassment and religious preference. Important cases in affirmative action include *University of California v Bakke, United Steelworkers of America v Weber*, and City of *Richmond v Croson*, and *Adarand Constructors v Pena*.

7 To ensure that organizations comply with antidiscrimination legislation, the Equal Employment Opportunity Commission (EEOC) was established to monitor employers' actions. Employers subject to federal laws must maintain records and report requested employment statistics where mandated. The Equal Employment Opportunity Commission maintains a complaint procedure for individuals who believe they have been discriminated against.

8 Affirmative action goes beyond providing equal employment opportunity to employees. Affirmative action requires employers to become more proactive and correct areas of past discrimination. This is accomplished by employing protected classes for jobs where they are underrepresented. The employer's goal is to have a balanced internal workforce representative of the employer's relevant labor market. In establishing an affirmative action plan, employers must (1) provide an organizational profile that graphically illustrates their workforce demographics, (2) establish goals and timetables for employment of underutilized protected classes, (3) develop actions and plans to reduce underutilization, including initiating proactive recruitment and selection methods, and (4) monitor progress of the entire affirmative action program.

REVIEW QUESTIONS

Multiple Choice
Choose the letter of the word or phrase that best completes each statement.

1. The treatment of individuals in all aspects of employment, hiring, promotion, training, etc. in a fair and nonbiased manner is
   a. equal employment opportunity.
   b. sexual harassment.
   c. age discrimination.
   d. the four-fifths rule.

2. A central aim of political action has been to establish justice for all people of the nation through the protection of
   a. United States Constitution.
   b. Fair Labor Standards.
   c. Equal Pay Act.
   d. Uniform Commercial Partnership Act.

3. Major federal EEO laws have attempted to correct social problems of interest to particular groups of workers called
   a. affirmative action.
   b. knowledge workers.
   c. protected classes.
   d. bona fide occupational qualification.

4. The act that outlaws discrimination in pay, employee benefits, and pensions based on the worker's gender is the
   a. Equal Employment Opportunity Act.
   b. Equal Pay Act.
   c. Age Discrimination in Employment Act.
   d. Americans with Disabilities Act.

5. The Civil Rights Act of 1964 and the Civil Rights Act of 1991 cover a broad range of organizations, **EXCEPT FOR**
   a. all private employers in interstate commerce who employ fifteen or more employees.
   b. all foreign organizations doing business in their domestic countries.
   c. state and local governments.
   d. private and public employment agencies, including the U.S. Employment Service.

6. Under Title VII of the Civil Rights Act, employers are permitted limited exemptions from anti-discrimination employment preferences based on a
   a. commercial code.
   b. past practice.
   c. common law.
   d. bona fide occupational qualification.

7. A practice that is necessary to the safe and efficient operation of the organization, interpreted by the courts is a defense based on
   a. religious preference.
   b. self-defense.
   c. business necessity.
   d. age discrimination.

8. The Pregnancy Discrimination Act affects employee benefit programs in the following ways **EXCEPT FOR**
   a. hospital and major medical insurance.
   b. vacation and holiday pay.
   c. temporary disability and salary continuation plans.
   d. sick leave policies.

9. An attempt by employees to adjust, without undue hardship, the working conditions or schedules of employees with disabilities or religious preferences is based on
   a. reasonable accommodation.
   b. labor contracts.
   c. fairness and inequities.
   d. job analysis.

10. Unwelcomed advances, requests for sexual favors, and other verbal or physical conduct of a sexual nature constitutes
   a. fraud.
   b. anti-discrimination.
   c. sexual harassment.
   d. misrepresentation of fact.

11. Illegal _____ has adversely affected welfare services and educational and Social Security benefits in the United States.
   a. protected classes
   b. immigration
   c. uniform guidelines
   d. bona fide occupational qualifications

12. An important procedural document for managers that applies to employee selection procedures in the areas of hiring, retention, promotion, transfer, demotion, dismissal, and referral is
    a. affirmative action.
    b. employee leasing.
    c. Uniform Guidelines.
    d. sexual harassment rules.

13. When using a test or other selection instrument to choose individuals for employment, employers must be able to prove
    a. affirmative action.
    b. adverse impact.
    c. disparate treatment.
    d. validity.

14. For an applicant or employee to pursue a discrimination case successfully, the individual must establish that the employer's selection procedures resulted in a(n)
    a. adverse impact on a protected class.
    b. undue process.
    c. affirmative action claim.
    d. violation of human rights.

15. As a rule of thumb to determine adverse impact in enforcement proceedings, the Equal Employment Opportunity Commission has adopted
    a. affirmative action procedures.
    b. the four-fifths rule.
    c. minimal wage provisions.
    d. overtime provisions.

16. The act of purposeful discrimination by an employer is called
    a. disparate treatment.
    b. adverse impact.
    c. antidiscrimination.
    d. bona fide occupational qualifications.

17. The type of analysis that will classify protected-class members by number and the type of job they hold within the organization is
    a. adverse impact.
    b. workforce utilization.
    c. business necessity.
    d. adverse treatment.

18. A benchmark case where the Supreme Court established two important principles – that discrimination need not be overt or intentional, and employment practices must be job-related - was
    a. Hopwood verses State of Texas.
    b. Albemarle Paper Company verses Moody.
    c. Wards Cove Packing Company verses Antonio.
    d. Griggs verses Duke Power Company.

19. The Court held that a statistical disparity among protected members of a workforce does not, in itself, show proof of discrimination was decided in the case of
    a. Griggs verses Duke Power Company.
    b. Albemarle Paper Company verses Moody.
    c. Wards Cove Packing Company verses Antonio.
    d. Hopwood verses State of Texas.

20. The commission that was created from Title VII of the Civil Rights law of 1964 was the
    a. Security Exchange Commission.
    b. Federal Trade Commission.
    c. Equal Employment Opportunity Commission
    d. Business Necessity Commission.

21. The filing of a discrimination charge form initiates an administrative procedure that can be lengthy, time-consuming, and costly for the
    a. employee.
    b. supervisor.
    c. labor union.
    d. employer.

22. The following are reasons why employers establish affirmative action programs, **EXCEPT FOR**
    a. provide an organizational profile that graphically illustrates their workforce demographics.
    b. establishing goals and timetables for employment of underutilized protected classes.
    c. monitor progress of the entire affirmative action program.
    d. develop a reactive strategy for recruitment and selection.

23. The act of giving preference to members of protected classes to the extent that unprotected individuals believe they are suffering discrimination is
    a. reverse discrimination.
    b. job analysis.
    c. job evaluation.
    d. performance appraisal.

24. One of the most famous reverse discrimination cases is
    a. Griggs verses Duke Power Company.
    b. University of California Regents verses Bakke
    c. Wards Cove Packing Company verses Antonio.
    d. Hopwood verses State of Texas.

25. Equal employment opportunity legislation requires managers to provide the same opportunities to
    a. customers and suppliers.
    b. all job applicants and employees regardless of ethnicity.
    c. business agents and labor unions.
    d. government agents and officials.

True/False

Identify the following statements as True or False.

1. Equal employment opportunity is a legal topic, however, it is not an emotional issue.

2. Equal employment opportunity as a national priority has emerged slowly in the United States.

3. The change in government and societal attitudes toward discrimination was further prompted by decreased public awareness of the economic imbalance between nonwhites and whites.

4. Since as early as the nineteenth century, the public has not been informed or aware of discriminatory employment practices in the United States.

5. Laws have been passed barring discrimination pertaining to recruitment, selection, performance appraisal, promotion, and compensation.

6. Employers violate the Equal Pay Act when differences in wages paid to men and women for equal work are based on seniority systems, merit considerations, or incentive pay plans.

7. Employers may defend their employment practices by a defense of bona fide occupational qualifications and/or business necessity.

8. Title VII of the Civil Rights Law of 1991 requires employers to grant complete religious freedom in employment situations.

9. Recent figures from the Equal Employment Opportunity Commission show that age discrimination complaints comprise about 20 percent of all discrimination charges.

10. Fair employment practices are state and local laws governing equal employment opportunity that are often less comprehensive than federal laws.

11. Quid pro quo sexual harassment can occur when unwelcome sexual conduct has the purpose or effect of unreasonably interfering with job performance.

12. In a hostile environment, sexual harassment can occur when submission to or rejection of sexual conduct is used as a basis for employment decisions.

13. Employers are completely certain about the appropriateness of specific selection procedures, especially those related to testing and selection.

14. Under the Uniform Guidelines, the use of any selection procedure, which has an adverse impact on the hiring, promotion, or other employment or membership opportunities of members of any race, sex, or ethnic group is considered to be discriminatory.

15. Adverse impact refers to the rejection for employment, placement, or promotion of a significantly lower percentage of a nonprotected class when compared with a protected class.

16. An alternative to population comparison rule, and one increasingly used in discrimination lawsuits, is to apply the 80/20 analysis to the observed applicant flow data.

17. Hiring individuals who must meet a minimum height or appearance standard (at the expense of protected class members) is evidence of a restricted policy by an employer.

18. The *Uniform Guidelines* have been given added importance through three leading Supreme Court cases; each case is noteworthy because it elaborates on the concepts of affirmative action, job enlargement, and job enrichment.

19. Equal Employment Opportunity Commission guidelines are not federal mandates by administrative rules and regulations published in the *Federal Register*.

20. Equal Employment Opportunity Commission investigations are conducted by fully trained equal opportunity specialists (EOSs) who have extensive experience in investigative procedures, theories of discrimination, and relief and remedy techniques.

21. Managers and supervisors must retaliate against individuals who invoke their legal rights to file charges or to support other employees during Equal Employment Opportunity Commission proceedings.

22. Since managers and supervisors are key to preventing and correcting discrimination; they, in particular, must be trained to understand employee rights and managerial obligations.

23. Affirmative action is achieved by having organizations follow specific guidelines and goals to ensure that they have a balanced and representative workforce.

24. Affirmative action as a national priority has been challenged because it has consistently resulted in the improvement in the employment status of protected groups.

25. Since the beginning of the 1990s, federal courts have decreasingly restricted the use of race and ethnicity in awarding scholarships, determining college admissions, making layoff decisions, selecting employees, promoting employees, and awarding government contracts.

Matching

Match each term with the proper definition.

Terms

a. adverse impact
b. affirmative action
c. bona fide occupational qualification (BFOQ)
d. business necessity
e charge form
f. disabled individual
g. disparate treatment
h. EEO-1 report

i. equal employment opportunity
j. fair employment practices (FEPs)
k. four-fifths rule
l. protected classes
m. reasonable accommodation
n. reverse discrimination
o. sexual harassment
p. *Uniform Guidelines on Employee Selection Procedures*
q. workforce utilization analysis

Definitions

_____ 1. any person who has a physical or mental impairment that substantially limits such person's major life activities

_____ 2. act of giving preference to members of protected classes to the extent that unprotected individuals believe they are suffering discrimination

_____ 3. the treatment of individuals in all aspects of employment - hiring, promotion, training, etc. - in a fair and nonbiased manner

_____ 4. individuals of a minority race, women, older persons, and those with disabilities who are covered by federal laws on equal employment opportunity

_____ 5. attempt by employers to adjust, without undue hardship, the working conditions or schedules of employees with disabilities or religious preferences

_____ 6. state and local laws governing equal employment opportunity that are often more comprehensive than federal laws

_____ 7. procedural document published in the Federal Register to assist employers in complying with federal regulations against discriminatory actions

_____   8. a concept that refers to the rejection of a significantly higher percentage
               of a protected class for employment, placement, or promotion when
               compared with the successful, nonprotected class

_____   9. rule of thumb followed by the Equal Employment Opportunity Commission
               in determining adverse impact in enforcement proceedings

_____   10. process of classifying protected class members by number and by the
               type of job they hold within the organization

_____   11. situation in which protected-class members receive unequal treatment or
               are evaluated by different standards

_____   12. unwelcome advances, requests for sexual favors, and other verbal or
               physical conduct of a sexual nature in the working environment

_____   13. suitable defense against a discrimination charge only where age, religion,
               sex, or national origin is an actual qualification for performing the job

_____   14. work-related practice that is necessary to the safe and efficient operation
               of an organization

_____   15. an employer information report that must be filed annually by employers
               of 100 or more employees (except state and local government employers)
               and government contractors and subcontractors to determine an
               employer's workforce composition

_____   16. discrimination complaint filed with the Equal Employment Opportunity
               Commission by employees or job applicants

_____   17. policy that goes beyond equal employment opportunity by requiring
               organizations to comply with the law and to correct past discriminatory
               practices by increasing the numbers of minorities and women in specific
               positions

Applications

1. The case of seven women against Arrowhead Bagel Co. brought what type of charges against management?
    a. sexual harassment and sexual assault.
    b. punishment and discipline.
    c. suspension and termination.
    d. oral warning and punitive damage.

2. In the case of TWA v Hardison, the Supreme Court ruled that employers need only make a reasonable accommodation for a current employee's or job applicant's
    a. union affiliation.
    b. employment vesting.
    c. religious observance.
    d. pension rights.

3. In a Supreme Court case, Toyota v Williams the court ruled that if physical or mental impairments are correctable then they are not a
    a. competitive reaction.
    b. disability.
    c. mental impairment.
    d. physical disease.

4. Griggs v Duke Power Co. was concerned with a minority meeting the qualifications of a position of a coal handler and exposed issues of
    a. sexual harassment.
    b. employment selection procedures.
    c. job burnout.
    d. employment fatigue.

5. Willie Griggs had applied for the position of coal handler with the Duke Power Company. His request for the position was denied because he was not a
    a. college graduate for the position in question.
    b. member of a protected class.
    c. business agent representing the local union.
    d. high school graduate, a requirement for the position.

How to Proceed with a Charge of Discrimination Against an Employer

Assume you are a minority student from a protected class. How could you charge an employer with discrimination if you are a candidate and denied employment on a job that has been advertised?

An individual may take a discrimination charge against an employer to the regional office of the Equal Employment Opportunity Commission or take the charge to the State Human Relations Commission.

An individual can bring forth a charge of adverse impact against an employer. This concept refers to the rejection of a significantly higher percentage of a protected class for employment, placement, or promotion when compared with the successful non-protected class of individuals. An individual can charge an employer with disparate treatment, which is a situation in which protected-class members receive unequal treatment or evaluated by different standards.

Individuals can bring forth a charge of the violation of the four-fifths rule against an employer, which is a rule of thumb followed by the Equal Employment Opportunity Commission in determining adverse impact for use in enforcement proceedings.

Any evidence that an employer has a selection procedure that excludes members of a protected class, whether intentional or not, constitutes adverse impact. Hiring individuals who must meet a minimum height or appearance standard (at the expense of protected class members) is evidence of such a restricted policy.

Individuals who believe they have been unjustly rejected for employment may demonstrate disparate treatment through the McDonnell Douglas test.

SOLUTIONS

Multiple Choice:	**True/False:**	**Matching:**
1. a	1. False	1. f
2. a	2. True	2. n
3. c	3. False	3. i
4. b	4. False	4. l
5. b	5. True	5. m
6. d	6. False	6. j
7. c	7. True	7. p
8. b	8. False	8. a
9. a	9. True	9. k
10. c	10. False	10. q
11. b	11. False	11. g
12. c	12. False	12. o
13. d	13. False	13. c
14. a	14. True	14. d
15. b	15. False	15. h
16. a	16. False	16. e
17. b	17. True	17. b
18. d	18. False	
19. c	19. True	
20. c	20. True	
21. d	21. False	
22. d	22. True	
23. a	23. True	
24. b	24. False	
25. b	25. False	

False Statements from True/False

1.   Equal employment opportunity is **not only** a legal topic, **it is also** an emotional issue.
3.   The change in government and societal attitudes toward discrimination was further prompted by **increasing** public awareness of the economic imbalance between nonwhites and whites.
4.   Since as early as the nineteenth century, the public **has been** aware of the discriminatory employment practices in the United States.
6.   Employers **do not** violate the Equal Pay Act when differences in wages paid to men and women for equal work are based on seniority systems, merit considerations, or incentive pay plans.
8.   Title VII of the Civil Rights Law of 1964 does **not** require employers to grant complete religious freedom in employment situations.

10. Fair employment practices are state and local laws governing equal employment opportunity that are often **more** comprehensive than federal laws.
11. **In a hostile environment, sexual harassment** can occur when unwelcome sexual conduct has the purpose or effect of unreasonably interfering with job performance.
12. **Quid pro quo sexual harassment** can occur when submission to or rejection of sexual conduct is used as a basis for employment decisions.
13. Employers are **often uncertain** about the appropriateness of specific selection procedures, especially those related to testing and selection.
15. Adverse impact refers to the rejection for employment, placement, or promotion of a significantly **higher** percentage of **a protected class** when compared with a **nonprotected class**.
16. An alternative to **four-fifths rule**, and one increasingly used in discrimination lawsuits, is to apply the **standard deviation** analysis to the observed applicant flow data.
18. The *Uniform Guidelines* **have been** given added importance through three leading Supreme Court cases, each case is noteworthy because it elaborates on the concepts of **adverse impact, validity testing, and job relatedness**.
21. Managers and supervisors must **not** retaliate against individuals who invoke their legal rights to file charges or to support other employees during Equal Employment Opportunity Commission proceedings.
24. Affirmative action as a national priority has been challenged because it **has not** consistently resulted in the improvement in the employment status of protected groups.
25. Since the beginning of the 1990s, federal courts have **increasingly** restricted the use of race and ethnicity in awarding scholarships, determining college admissions, making layoff decisions, selecting employees, promoting employees, and awarding government contracts.

Applications

1. a
2. c
3. b
4. b
5. d

CHAPTER 3

JOB ANALYSIS, EMPLOYEE INVOLVEMENT, AND FLEXIBLE WORK SCHEDULES

In this chapter you will learn the relationship between job requirements and the performance of human resources management functions. As a student you will learn that job requirements provide the foundation on which many human resources decisions, including those relating to recruitment, selection, training, evaluation, and compensation, must be based. It is essential that the requirements of each job in the organization are determined accurately. Supervisors and their employees must be aware of these job requirements. You will learn the relevance of job analysis and how it is used to write job descriptions and job specifications.

You will also understand the different techniques used to maximize employee contributions, be able to discuss the various job characteristics that motivate employees, and finally, how managers can implement alternative work schedules.

LEARNING OBJECTIVES

After studying this chapter you should be able to

 Discuss the relationship between job requirements and the performance of human resources management functions.

 Indicate the methods by which job analysis typically is completed.

 Identify and explain the various sections of job descriptions.

 Provide examples illustrating the various factors that must be taken into account in redesigning a job.

 Discuss the various job characteristics that motivate employees.

Describe the different group techniques used to maximize employee contributions.

Differentiate and explain the different adjustments in work schedules.

CHAPTER SUMMARY RELATING TO LEARNING OBJECTIVES

Job requirements reflect the different duties, tasks, and responsibilities contained in jobs. Job requirements, in turn, influence the human resources function performed by managers, including recruitment, selection, training and development, performance appraisal, compensation, and various labor relations activities.

Job analysis data may be gathered using one of several collection methods interviews, questionnaires, observations, or diaries. Other more quantitative approaches include use of the functional job analysis, the position analysis questionnaire system, and the critical incident method. It is the prevailing opinion of the courts that human resources management decisions on employment, performance appraisal, and promotions must be based on specific criteria that are job-related. These criteria can be determined objectively only by analyzing the requirements of each job.

The format of job descriptions varies widely, often reflecting the needs of the organization and the expertise of the writer. As a minimum, job descriptions should contain a job title, a job identification section, and an essential function section. A job specification section also may be included. Job descriptions should be written in clear and specific terms with consideration given to their legal implications.

Job design is a combination of four basic considerations: organizational objectives; industrial engineering concerns of analyzing work methods and establishing time standards; ergonomic considerations, which accommodate human capabilities and limitations to job tasks; and employee contributions.

In the job characteristics' model, five job factors contribute to increased job performance and satisfaction skill task variety, task identity, task significance, autonomy, and feedback. All factors should be built into jobs since each factor influences different employee psychological states. When jobs are enriched in the job characteristic model, then employees experience more meaningfulness in their jobs, they acquire more job responsibility, and they receive direct feedback from the tasks they perform.

6 To improve the internal process of organizations and increase American Productivity, greater efforts are being made by organizations to enhance employee contributions to work operations. Employee involvement groups are composed of employees in work units charged with offering suggestions for improving productivity or service quality or fostering workplace effectiveness. Employee teams stress employee collaboration over individual accomplishment. The result of this is a synergistic outgrowth of the team. Teams rely on the expertise and different abilities of members to achieve a specific goal or objective. Self-directed teams are characterized by their willingness to perform traditional managerial tasks.

7 Changes in work schedules - which include the compressed workweek, flextime job sharing, and telecommuting - permit employees to adjust their work periods to accommodate their particular lifestyles. Employees can select from among these human resources techniques to accommodate diverse employee needs while fostering organizational effectiveness.

REVIEW QUESTIONS

Multiple Choice

Choose the letter of the word or phrase that best completes each statement.

1 _____ 1. A group of related activities and duties is a
                       a. job.
                       b. position.
                       c. salary range.
                       d. pay grade.

1 _____ 2   The function that consists of different duties and responsibilities performed by only one employee is a
                       a. job.
                       b. position.
                       c. salary range.
                       d. pay grade.

1 _____ 3. The purposes of recruitment, training, compensation, or advancement opportunities may be grouped into a
                       a. position description.
                       b. job enlargement.
                       c. job analysis.
                       d. job family.

objective 1

_____ 4. Before capable employees can be found for an organization, recruiters need to know the
   a. critical incident method.
   b. job specifications.
   c. job analysis method.
   d. participant diary log.

objective 1

_____ 5. Job specifications establish the qualifications required of applicants. It serves an essential role in the
   a. recruiting function.
   b. functional job analysis.
   c. job characteristics model.
   d. production function.

objective 1

_____ 6. A statement of the tasks, duties, and responsibilities of a job is a
   a. job family.
   b. job specification.
   c. job description.
   d. position.

objective 2

_____ 7. Human resources managers use job analysis data to develop
   a. attitude and behavior surveys.
   b. job descriptions and job specifications.
   c. functional job analysis and ergonomics issues.
   d. employee and labor union contracts.

objective 2

_____ 8. Accurate job data must be collected from employees in order to create an effective
   a. affirmative action program.
   b. job analysis.
   c. employer association.
   d. quota system.

objective 2

_____ 9. The job analysis technique that is worker-oriented and covers 194 different tasks is
   a. task inventory development.
   b. the critical incident method.
   c. functional job analysis.
   d. the position analysis questionnaire.

objective 3

_____ 10. Most job descriptions contain all of the following **EXCEPT FOR**
   a. job title.
   b. job identification.
   c. job duties section.
   d. job evaluation section.

11. From the employee's standpoint, written _____ can minimize
    the misunderstandings that occur between managers and their
    subordinates concerning job requirements.
    a. job specifications
    b. position analysis questionnaires
    c. job descriptions
    d. critical incidences

12. The section of a job description that provides information about
    the location of the job and the reporting relationships involved is
    the
    a. job identification section.
    b. job duty section.
    c. job title.
    d. job specifications.

13. The term that describes the process that is concerned with
    structuring jobs in order to improve the organization's efficiency
    and employee satisfaction is
    a. job specification.
    b. job analysis.
    c. job design.
    d. job selection.

14. In order to capture the talents of employees while improving
    organization performance job design is concerned with
    a. modifying jobs.
    b. changing jobs.
    c. enriching jobs.
    d. all of the above.

15. Any effort that makes work more rewarding or satisfying by adding
    more meaningful tasks to an employee's job is
    a. job enlargement.
    b. job specification.
    c. job enrichment.
    d. job analysis.

16. Herzberg developed the concept of fulfilling employee needs such
    as self-fulfillment and self-esteem while achieving long-term job
    satisfaction and performance goals is known as
    a. job enlargement.
    b. job specification.
    c. job enrichment.
    d. job analysis.

5 _____ 17. The following are traits in the job characteristics' model **EXCEPT FOR**
   a. skill variety.
   b. task identity.
   c. task significance.
   d. consensus decision-making.

5 _____ 18. A technique of involving employees in their work through the process of inclusion is
   a. employee empowerment.
   b. employee downsizing.
   c. job enlargement.
   d. re-engineering of work.

5 _____ 19. The process that attempts to accommodate the human capabilities and limitations of those who are to perform a job is
   a. job analysis.
   b. job enrichment.
   c. ergonomics.
   d. job enlargement.

6 _____ 20. Those participating in employee involvement groups (EIs) must receive comprehensive training in problem identification, problem analysis, and various decision-making tools such as
   a. program and non-program decisions.
   b. quality circles and self-managed teams.
   c. centralized and decentralized authority.
   d. statistical analysis and cause-and-effect diagrams.

6 _____ 21. A logical outgrowth of employment involvement work groups and the philosophy of employee empowerment would be
   a. labor unions.
   b. informal groups of employees.
   c. employee teams.
   d. temporary work groups.

7 _____ 22. Advanced computer and telecommunications technology to link team members who are geographically dispersed – often worldwide – are
   a. employee involvement groups.
   b. virtual teams.
   c. job analysis.
   d. flextime workers.

7 _____ 23. From the employer's standpoint, flextime can be most helpful in
             a. predicting employee turnover.
             b. recruiting and retaining personnel.
             c. developing job sharing.
             d. flexible and adaptable work schedules.

7 _____ 24. The arrangement whereby two part-time employees perform a job
             that otherwise would be held by one-full-time employee is called
             a. job sharing.
             b. job rotation.
             c. flextime.
             d. flexible schedules.

7 _____ 25. The following are disadvantages to flextime **EXCEPT FOR**
             a. It improves service to customers/clients by extending
                operating hours.
             b. It is not suited for some jobs.
             c. It creates communications problems for managers and
                employees.
             d. Managers may have to extend their workweek.

True/False

Identify the following statements as True or False.

1 _____ 1. Any discrepancies between the knowledge, skills, and abilities
            demonstrated by a jobholder and the requirements contained in
            the description and specification for that job provide clues to
            training needs.

1 _____ 2. The requirements contained in the description of a job provide the
            criteria for appraising the performance of the holder of that job is
            called job evaluation.

1 _____ 3. In determining the rate to be paid for performing a job, the relative
            worth of the job would be the least important factor to be
            considered.

2 _____ 4. Job analysis is the process of obtaining information about jobs by
            determining what the duties, tasks, or activities of those jobs are.

5. The job description and job specifications developed through job analysis should be as inaccurate as possible if they are to be of value to those who make Human Resources Management (HRM) decisions.

6. Common methods of analyzing jobs when undertaking job analysis would include interviews, questionnaires, observation, and diaries.

7. Developed by the U.S. Training and Employment Service, the functional job analysis (FJA) approach utilizes an inventory of the various types of functions or work activities that can constitute any job.

8. The objective of the critical incident method when undertaking job analysis is to identify 194 items in the checklist of the position analysis questionnaire.

9. In writing a job description, selection of a job title is important in providing status to the employee, such as "sanitation engineer" is preferred as to "garbage collector."

10. Skills that are irrelevant to a job include education, social interaction, specialized training, personal traits or abilities and family dexterities.

11. When writing a job description, it is essential to use statements that are loose, vague, and comprehensive.

12. There are two job design methods, job enrichment and job characteristic, which seek to incorporate the behavioral needs of employees as they perform their individual jobs.

13. Job enlargement or the vertical expansion of jobs, may be accomplished by increasing the autonomy and responsibility of employees.

14. According to Richard Hackman and Greg Oldham, their job characteristics model proposes that three psychological states of a jobholder result in improved work performance, internal motivation, and lower absenteeism and turnover.

15. Empowerment encourages employees to become innovators and managers of their own work, and it involves them in their jobs in ways that give them more control and autonomous decision-making.

5
_____ 16. The outgrowth of scientific management was industrial engineering, which is concerned with analyzing work methods and establishing time standards.

5
_____ 17. Ergonomics is concerned with equipment design and must only take into consideration the mental ability of operators to use the equipment and to react through vision, hearing, and touch to the information the equipment conveys.

5
_____ 18. Ergonomics has recently focused on the increase and inclusion of many repetitive motion injuries, particularly those related to the back and wrist.

6
_____ 19. Designing work to enhance group or worker productivity includes the techniques of collaboration and synergy.

6
_____ 20. Permanent groups of five to ten employees doing similar or related work who meet together regularly to identify, analyze, and suggest solutions to shared problems are often referred to as a task force.

6
_____ 21. The concept of job enrichment occurs when the interaction and outcome of team members is greater than the sum of their individual efforts.

6
_____ 22. Work teams can operate in a variety of organization structures, each with different strategic purposes or functional activities.

7
_____ 23. Flextime or flexible working hours permits employees the option of choosing daily starting and quitting times, provided that they work a certain number of hours per day or week.

7
_____ 24. Telecommuting is the use of personal computers, networks and other communications technology such as fax machines to do work in the home that is traditionally done in the workplace.

7
_____ 25. A variant of telecommunicating is the cyber workspace where employees are in the office selling to, or servicing, customers or stationed at other remote locations working as if they were in the field.

Matching

Match each term with the proper definition.

Terms

a. critical incident method
b. employee empowerment
c. employee involvement groups (EIs)
d. employee teams
e. ergonomics
f. flextime
g. functional job analysis (FJA)
h. industrial engineering
i. job
j. job analysis

k. job characteristics model
l. job description
m. job design
n. job enrichment
o. job family
p. job specification
q. position
r. position analysis questionnaire(PAQ)
s. telecommuting
t. virtual team

Definitions

_____ 1. flexible working hours that give employees the option of choosing daily starting and quitting times, provided that they work a set number of hours per day or week

_____ 2. empowerment approach that purports that improving the psychological state of a jobholder results in improved work performance, internal motivation, and lower absenteeism and turnover

_____ 3. statement of the needed knowledge, skills, and abilities of the person who is to perform the job

_____ 4. where different jobs have similar duties and responsibilities

_____ 5. granting employees power to initiate change, thereby encouraging them to take charge of what they do

_____ 6. use of personal computers, networks, and other communications technology to do work in the home that has traditionally been done in the workplace

_____ 7. outgrowth of job analysis that improves jobs is concerned with structuring jobs in order to improve organization efficiency and employee job satisfaction

_____ 8. a field of study concerned with analyzing work methods and establishing time standards

_____ 9. logical outgrowth of employee involvement and the philosophy of empowerment

_____ 10. an interdisciplinary approach to equipment and systems that can be easily and efficiently used by employees

_____ 11. the different duties and responsibilities performed by a single employee

_____ 12. job analysis method in which important job tasks are identified for job success

_____ 13. process of obtaining information about a job by determining the job's duties, tasks, or activities

_____ 14. enhancing a job by adding more meaningful tasks and duties to make the work more rewarding or satisfying

_____ 15. quantitative approach to job analysis that involves compiling an inventory of the various functions or work activities of a job and that assumes that each job involves three broad worker functions: data, people, and things

_____ 16. questionnaire covering 194 different tasks which, by means of a five-point scale, seeks to determine the degree to which different tasks are involved in performing a particular job

_____ 17. a group of related activities and duties

_____ 18. groups of employees who meet to resolve problems or offer suggestions for organizational improvement

_____ 19. a team with widely dispersed members linked together through computer and telecommunications technology.

_____ 20. statement of a job's tasks, duties, and responsibilities

Applications

🖐️5 _____ 1. In today's highly competitive and dynamic business environment employers as diverse as Home Depot, Wal-Mart, Cigna Health Care, Costco, Auto Zone, Disney, and Applebee's have turned to their employees to improve
   a. job specifications.
   b. organizational performance.
   c. position descriptions.
   d. job analysis.

2. A cost effective process that organizations such as Compaq Computer, 3M, Pratt and Whitney, and the U.S. Postal Service is
   a. ergonomics.
   b. human resource planning.
   c. job analysis.
   d. total quality management.

3. At organizations such as Federal Express, Hewlett-Packard, the City of Phoenix, and Calvin Klein more integration of individual skills, better performance in terms of quality and quantity, and reduced delivery time are benefits from
   a. employer association.
   b. employee teams.
   c. affirmative action programs.
   d. sexual harassment.

4. The president of Organizational Renaissance noted concerns of language and cultural barriers, conflicts due to diverse geographical locations, selecting people who are self-starters and have technological skills, and behavioral problems caused by lack of close interpersonal contact involving the use of
   a. virtual teams.
   b. employee assistance programs.
   c. employee diversification.
   d. labor unions.

5. Sentry Insurance Company has found a way to reduce traditional causes of tardiness and absenteeism through the use of
   a. flextime.
   b. virtual reality.
   c. employee assistance programs.
   d. total quality management.

How To Inquire About a Realistic Job Preview

A student may inquire how to pursue a realistic job preview when interviewing with an employer or the Human Resources Department.

A line manager or the Human Resources Department should state a realistic job preview in every interview. This process is an accurate portrayal of the job description that one is expected to perform. It would include the job title, duties and responsibilities, and the authority delegated in the performance of a job. Opportunities for growth and a career development program should be discussed to provide the fullest amount of information to each job applicant applying for a position. Remember it is the responsibility of the individual applying for a job or the employee to initiate the discussion of a career development program. One can inquire about a job specification, which outlines the minimal qualifications required in filling a job. A job specification pertains to the abilities and skills required to perform a job. It includes the educational requirement and work experience necessary in the recruiting efforts of the Human Resources Department. Note: one should attempt to match up these job requirements to their own strengths.

SOLUTIONS

Multiple Choice:	True/False:	Matching:
1. a	1. True	1. f
2. b	2. False	2. k
3. d	3. False	3. p
4. b	4. True	4. o
5. a	5. False	5. b
6. c	6. True	6. s
7. b	7. True	7. m
8. b	8. False	8. h
9. d	9. True	9. d
10. d	10. False	10. e
11. c	11. False	11. q
12. a	12. True	12. a
13. c	13. False	13. j
14. d	14. True	14. n
15. c	15. True	15. g
16. c	16. True	16. r
17. d	17. False	17. i
18. a	18. False	18. c
19. c	19. True	19. t
20. d	20. False	20. l
21. c	21. False	
22. b	22. True	
23. b	23. True	
24. a	24. True	
25. a	25. False	

False Statements from True/False

2. The requirements contained in the description of a job provide the criteria for **evaluating the performance of the holder of that job is called a performance appraisal**.
3. In determining the rate to be paid for performing a job, the relative worth of the job is one of the **most** important factors.
5. The job descriptions and job specifications developed through job analysis should be as **accurate** as possible if they are to be of value to those who make human resources management decisions.
8. The objective of the critical incident method **is to identify critical job tasks**.
10. Skills that are **relevant** to a job include education or **experience**, specialized training, personal traits or abilities, and **manual** dexterities.
11. When writing a job description, it is essential to use statements that are **terse, direct, and simply worded**.

13. Job **enrichment**, or the vertical expansion of jobs, may be accomplished by increasing the autonomy and responsibility of employees.
17. Ergonomics **attempts to accommodate the human capabilities and limitations of those who are to perform a job. It is concerned with adapting the entire job system—the work, the work environment, the machine and equipment, and the processes—to match human characteristics**.
18. Ergonomics has recently focused on the **elimination, or at least the reduction**, of many repetitive motion injuries, particularly those related to the back and wrist.
20. Permanent groups of five to ten employees doing similar or related work who meet together regularly to identify, analyze, and suggest solutions to shared problems are often referred to as **employee involvement groups**.
21. The concept of **synergy** occurs when the interaction and outcome of team members is greater than the sum of their individual efforts.
25. A variant of telecommunicating is the **virtual office** where employees are in the **field** selling to, or servicing, customers or stationed at other remote locations working as if they were in the **home office**.

Applications

1. b
2. a
3. b
4. a
5. a

CHAPTER 4

HUMAN RESOURCES PLANNING AND RECRUITMENT

In this chapter you will learn an effective human resources management program requires staffing needs to be anticipated sufficiently in advance to permit the recruitment and development of fully qualified personnel. You will understand how human resources planning (HRP) must be coordinated closely with planning for the other functions being performed, as well as with planning for the organization as a whole. Finally, you will know that human resources planning thus provides the basis for determining specific recruitment needs for each department within the organization. Keep in mind recruitment activities is integrated with diversity and equal employment opportunity initiatives.

LEARNING OBJECTIVES

After studying this chapter you should be able to

 Identify the advantages of integrating human resources planning and strategic planning.

 Describe the basic approaches to human resources planning.

 Explain the advantages and disadvantages of recruiting from within the organization.

 Explain the advantages and disadvantages of external recruitment.

 Describe how recruitment activities are integrated with diversity and equal employment opportunity initiatives.

CHAPTER SUMMARY RELATING TO LEARNING OBJECTIVES

1 As organizations plan for their future, top management and strategic planners must recognize that strategic-planning decisions affect and are affected by human resources functions. On the one hand, human resources planning plays a proactive role in making certain the right number and type of employees are available to implement a chosen business plan. On the other hand, human resources planning can proactively identify and initiate programs needed to develop organizational capabilities upon which future strategies can be built.

2 Human resources planning is a systematic process that involves forecasting demand for labor, performing supply analysis, and balancing supply and demand considerations. Forecasting demand requires using either quantitative or qualitative methods to identify the number and type of people needed to meet organizational objectives. Supply analysis involves determining if there are sufficient employees available within the organization to meet demand and also determining whether potential employees are available in the job market. Reconciling supply and demand requires a host of activities, including internal and external recruitment.

3 Employers usually find it advantageous to use internal promotion and transfer to fill as many openings as possible above the entry level. By recruiting from within, an organization can capitalize on previous investments made in recruiting, selecting, training, and developing its current employees. Further, internal promotions can reward employees for past performance and send a signal to other employees that their future efforts will pay off. However, potential candidates from the outside should occasionally be considered in order to prevent the inbreeding of ideas and attitudes.

4 Filling jobs above the entry level often requires managers to rely upon outside sources. These outside sources are also utilized to fill jobs with special qualifications, to avoid excessive inbreeding, and to acquire new ideas and technology. Which outside sources and methods are used in recruiting will depend on the recruitment goals of the organization, the conditions of the labor market, and the specifications of the jobs to be filled.

5 The legal requirements governing equal employment opportunity make it mandatory that employers exert a positive effort to recruit and promote members of protected classes so that their representation at all levels within the organization will approximate their proportionate numbers in the local labor market. These efforts include recruiting not only those members who are qualified, but also those who can become qualified with reasonable training and assistance.

REVIEW QUESTIONS

Multiple Choice

Choose the letter of the word or phrase that best completes each statement.

1. Human resources planning is
   a. a technique that identifies the critical aspects of a job.
   b. the process of anticipating and making provision for movement of people into, within, and out of an organization.
   c. the process of setting major organizational objectives and developing comprehensive plans to achieve these objectives.
   d. the process of determining the primary direction of the firm.

2. In planning for the future of an organization as a whole, managers must be concerned with meshing
   a. organization and labor unions.
   b. mechanistic and organic concerns.
   c. human resources planning and strategic planning.
   d. joint ventures and subsidiaries.

3. Human resources planning and strategic planning are linked in the following ways
   a. linking the planning processes.
   b. mapping an organization's human capital architecture.
   c. ensuring fit and flexibility.
   d. all of the above.

4. The capacity of the organization to act and change in pursuit of sustainable competitive advantage is
   a. recruiting.
   b. organizational capability.
   c. human resources planning.
   d. production capacity.

5. The systematic monitoring of the major external forces influencing the organization is
   a. re-engineering.
   b. environmental scanning.
   c. human resources planning.
   d. management forecasting.

6. The process of examining the culture and quality of work life in an organization is a
    a. cultural audit.
    b. human resources planning plan.
    c. job enlargement.
    d. job analysis.

7. The process of identifying the "best practice" in a given industry and then comparing the companies' practices to the industries "best practice" is
    a. reengineering.
    b. job analysis.
    c. performance appraisal.
    d. benchmarking.

8. The two approaches used in human resources forecasting are
    a. labor market turnover and yield ratio forecasts.
    b. the Markov model and employee leasing forecasts.
    c. the replacement chart and skilled inventories forecasts.
    d. qualitative and quantitative forecasts.

9. The opinions (judgments) of supervisors, department managers, experts, or others knowledgeable about the organization's future employment needs is
    a. management forecasts.
    b. human resources planning.
    c. leading and controlling resources.
    d. computer networks.

10. A list of current jobholders and potential candidates if openings occur is a
    a. job analysis.
    b. job description.
    c. job specification.
    d. replacement chart.

11. The process of identifying, developing, and tracking key individuals for executive positions is
    a. succession planning.
    b. organizational capacity.
    c. realistic job previews.
    d. benchmarking.

12. The determination of where and how candidates with the required qualifications are to be found to fill vacancies is
    a. demand considerations.
    b. supply considerations.
    c. job enlargement.
    d. human resources planning.

13. A long-term process of restructuring organizations to minimize costs is
    a. downsizing the organization.
    b. reengineering jobs.
    c. work diversification.
    d. proceeding with job analysis.

14. Most organizations try to follow a policy of filling job vacancies above the entry-level position through
    a. supply analysis and yield ratios.
    b. nepotism and replacement charts.
    c. trend analysis and skill inventories.
    d. promotions and transfers.

15. Methods that enable organizations to locate qualified job candidates within the organization include the following **EXCEPT FOR**
    a. job posting.
    b. recall of laid-off employees.
    c. computerized record systems.
    d. word of mouth.

16. Managers can access human resource information and identify potential internal candidates for available jobs through
    a. public employment agencies.
    b. user-friendly search engines.
    c. colleges and universities.
    d. private employment agencies.

17. The method that makes websites available where applicants can submit their resumes and potential employers can check for qualified applicants is
    a. local area networks.
    b. network programming.
    c. internet recruiting.
    d. realistic job previews.

18. Recommendations made by current employees to fill internal employment positions are
    a. temporary employees.
    b. employee referrals.
    c. casual employment.
    d. employee leasing.

19. The practice of hiring relatives in employment positions is referred to as
    a. nepotism.
    b. affirmative action.
    c. human resources planning.
    d. hiring from a protected class.

20. Instead of helping job seekers find the right job, these organizations concentrate on helping employers find the right person for a job.
    a. executive search firms
    b. U.S. Department of Labor
    c. Bureau of Employment Security
    d. public employment agencies

21. Employees who are used for short-term assignments and/or help when managers cannot justify hiring a full-time employee, such as for vacation fill-ins are
    a. probationary employees.
    b. leased employees.
    c. temporary employees.
    d. permanent employees.

22. A process that informs applicants about all aspects of a job, including both its desirable and undesirable facets is a(n)
    a. job analysis.
    b. realistic job preview
    c. job specification.
    d. affirmative action program.

23. The largest numbers among protected classes that account for 48 percent of all positions in management and professional occupations are
    a. Hispanics.
    b. African Americans.
    c. women.
    d. men.

_5_   _____   24. The most frequently cited advantages of employing disabled persons include the following, **EXCEPT FOR**
  a. dependability.
  b. superior attendance.
  c. loyalty.
  d. high turnover.

_5_   _____   25. An excellent recruitment source for staffing part-time and full-time positions that are otherwise hard to fill are
  a. teenagers.
  b. permanent employees.
  c. older individuals.
  d. leased employees.

True/False

Identify the following statements as True or False.

_1_   _____   1. Evidence suggests that employers are finding it easier to staff jobs ranging from the unskilled to the professional and highly technical.

_1_   _____   2. In the next decade, the fastest-growing segments of the workforce will be Asian Americans and Hispanics.

_1_   _____   3. Lack of human resources planning can make it difficult for employees to make effective plans for career or personal development.

_1_   _____   4. Human resources managers are important facilitators of the planning process and are viewed as credible and important contributors to creating the organization's future.

_1_   _____   5. Underlying a firm's core competencies is a portfolio of assets, liabilities, and owner's equity.

_1_   _____   6. An increasingly vital element of realistic job previews is determining whether people are available, internally or externally, to carry out the organization's strategies.

_1_   _____   7. External fit or alignment focuses on the connection between the business objectives and the major initiatives in human resources.

8. Resource flexibility results from having people who can do many different things in different ways.

9. A variety of organizational factors, including competitive strategy, technology, structure, and productivity, can influence the demand for labor.

10. Forecasting is frequently more an art than a science, providing inexact approximations rather than absolute results.

11. The target company for benchmarking must be a competitor.

12. Qualitative human resources forecasting techniques generally employ sophisticated analytical models.

13. Quantitative approaches to forecasting involve the use of statistical or mathematical techniques.

14. Over the past decade, early retirements have become a more common means for organizations to reduce excess labor supply.

15. Transfers usually provide the same motivational value as promotions.

16. Applicants who find employment through referral by a current employee tend to remain with the organization for a shorter time and give lower-quality performance than those employees recruited through the formal recruitment sources of advertisements and employment agencies.

17. The most common method of attracting applicants is through nepotism.

18. It is estimated that nine out of ten U.S. companies, including both large and small firms, make some use of temporary employees.

19. Unlike temporary employment agencies, employee-leasing companies place their employees with subscribers on a permanent basis.

20. Yield ratios help indicate which recruitment sources are least effective at producing qualified job candidates.

4
objective
_____ 21. Regardless of who does the recruiting, it is imperative that these individuals have a good understanding of the knowledge, skills, abilities, experiences, and other characteristics required for the job.

5
objective
_____ 22. An essential part of any equal employment opportunity or affirmative action policy must be an affirmative effort to recruit members of non-protected classes.

5
objective
_____ 23. According to the text, over 60 percent of all women in the workforce have been responsible for supporting themselves, and three out of five of them are heads of households.

5
objective
_____ 24. For many minorities employment opportunities still remain exceedingly unlimited because of educational and societal disadvantages.

5
objective
_____ 25. The lack of special facilities for physically impaired persons, those in wheelchairs, has been a further employment restriction.

Matching

Match each term with the proper definition.

Terms

a. benchmarking
b. core knowledge workers
c. cultural audits
d. demand considerations
e. employee leasing
f. human resources planning (HRP)
g. job posting and bidding
h. labor market
i. management forecasts
j. Markov analysis

k. nepotism
l. organizational capability
m. realistic job preview (RJP)
n. replacement charts
o. skill inventories
p. staffing tables
q. succession planning
r. supply considerations
s. trend analysis
t. yield ratio

Definitions

_____ 1. forecasts employment requirements on the basis of some organizational index

_____ 2. the process of identifying, developing, and tracking key individuals so that they may eventually assume top-level positions

_____ 3. graphic representations of all organizational jobs, along with the numbers of employees currently occupying those jobs, and future employment requirements

_____ 4. the capacity of the organization to act and change in pursuit of sustainable competitive advantage

_____ 5. places employees with subscribers on a permanent basis

_____ 6. list current jobholders and identify possible replacements should openings occur

_____ 7. the area from which applicants are to be recruited

_____ 8. the practice of hiring relatives

_____ 9. the opinions of supervisors, department managers, experts, or others knowledgeable about the organization's future employment needs

_____ 10. percentage of applicants from a particular source that make it to the next stage in the selection process

_____ 11. the process that consists largely of posting vacancy notices on bulletin boards, but may also include use of designated posting centers, employee publications, special handouts, direct mail, and public-address messages

_____ 12. the process of anticipating and making provision for the movement of people into, within, and out of an organization

_____ 13. list each employee's education, past work experience, vocational interests, specific abilities and skills, compensation history, and job tenure

_____ 14. examine the attitudes and activities of the workforce

_____ 15. shows the percentage and actual number of employees, who remain in each job from one year to the next, as well as the proportions of those who are promoted, demoted, transferred, or exit the organization

_____ 16. informs an applicant about all aspects of the job, including both its desirable and undesirable aspects

_____ 17. based on forecasted trends in business activity

_____18. process of identifying the "best practice" in a given industry, and then comparing the companies' practices to the "best practice"

_____19. group of employees who have firm-specific skills that are directly linked to the company's strategy

_____20. the determination of where and how candidates with the required qualifications are to be found to fill vacancies

Applications

_____ 1. In the best of companies such as Fairmont Hotels, GE, and IBM, there is virtually no distinction between strategic planning and
a. strategic alliances.
b. labor union goals.
c. human resources planning.
d. operating plans.

_____ 2. Organizations like Zenith Data Systems, Westinghouse, and the State of Illinois use computers and special programs to compile data for
a. replacement cards.
b. skill inventories.
c. data processing cards.
d. programming cards.

_____ 3. To promote high morale, firms such as Marriott and Nordstrom, advocate a policy of
a. external recruiting.
b. hiring from the competition.
c. hiring lobbyist.
d. promotion from within.

_____ 4. To fill top-management positions, firms such as Texaco, Pillsbury, and MONEY Financial Services use
a. temporary agencies.
b. executive search firms.
c. public employment agencies.
d. referrals and walk-ins.

5. To find experienced workers, Home Shopping Network, a
    24-hour-a-day cable television company, located its headquarters
    in Florida in order to recruit
    a. older workers.
    b. younger individuals.
    c. migrant workers.
    d. foreign applicants.

How to Write a Resume and Search for a Job

How to prepare and market oneself for a job before graduating from your educational
institution.

Most colleges and universities have a placement office, and you should contact this
office before graduation. Some of the services provided by this office are as follows:
*   resume writing.
*   portfolio development.
*   interview coaching.
*   how to tap the hidden job market.
*   how to job search using the internet.
Before graduation you should inquire about cooperative education to gain field
experience through an internship, externship, practicum, clinical, and other job related
experiences. It is difficult for a student to market a degree without any field experience.

You should attend workshops, annual job fairs, and career counseling services before
graduation.

A job requisition booklet should be reviewed and analyzed before you enter the labor
market. Remember that it is your responsibility to contact the placement office at your
school, so that they may assist in your career development program.

SOLUTIONS

Multiple Choice:	**True/False:**	**Matching:**
1. b	1. False	1. s
2. c	2. True	2. q
3. d	3. True	3. p
4. b	4. True	4. l
5. b	5. False	5. e
6. a	6. False	6. n
7. d	7. True	7. h
8. d	8. True	8. k
9. a	9. True	9. i
10. d	10. True	10. t
11. a	11. False	11. g
12. b	12. False	12. f
13. a	13. True	13. o
14. d	14. True	14. c
15. d	15. False	15. j
16. b	16. False	16. m
17. c	17. False	17. d
18. b	18. True	18. a
19. a	19. True	19. b
20. a	20. False	20. r
21. c	21. True	
22. b	22. False	
23. c	23. True	
24. d	24. False	
25. c	25. True	

False Statements from True/False

1. Evidence suggests that employers **having difficulty** staff jobs ranging from the unskilled to the professional and highly technical.
5. Underlying a firm's core competencies is a portfolio of **employee skills and human capital**.
6. An increasingly vital element of **strategic planning** is determining whether people are available, internally or externally, to carry out the organization's strategies.
11. The target company for benchmarking **does not need to be** a competitor.
12. **Quantitative** human resources forecasting techniques generally employ sophisticated analytical models.
15. Transfers usually **lack** the same motivational value as promotions.

16. Applicants who find employment through referral by a current employee tend to remain with the organization for a **longer** time and give **higher**-quality performance than those employees recruited through the formal recruitment sources of advertisements and employment agencies.

17. **One of the** most common methods of attracting applicants is through **advertisements**.

20. Yield ratios help indicate which recruitment sources are **most** effective at producing qualified job candidates.

22. An essential part of any equal employment opportunity or affirmative action policy must be an affirmative effort to recruit members of **protected** classes.

24. For many minorities employment opportunities still remain exceedingly **limited** because of educational and societal disadvantages.

Applications

1. c
2. b
3. d
4. b
5. a

CHAPTER 5

SELECTION

This chapter emphasizes the importance of personnel selection in the building of a productive workforce. Determining the qualifications of job candidates requires that as much information as possible is obtained from the candidates and other sources. One should know such information should be relevant to the job and sufficiently reliable and valid. It is essential that interviewers are thoroughly trained in how to obtain the information needed and how to avoid being discriminatory. Human Resources practitioners should have an understanding of job requirements to permit an analysis of application forms, employment tests, interviews, and reference checks of individual candidates.

LEARNING OBJECTIVES

After studying this chapter you should be able to

 Explain the objectives of the personnel selection process.

 Identify the various sources of information used for personnel selection.

 Compare the value of different types of employment tests.

 Illustrate the different approaches to conducting an employment interview.

 Describe the various decision strategies for selection undertaken by the organization.

CHAPTER SUMMARY RELATING TO LEARNING OBJECTIVES

1 The selection process should provide as much reliable and valid information as possible about applicants so that their qualifications can be carefully matched with job specifications. The information that is obtained should be clearly job-related or predictive of success on the job and free from potential discrimination. Reliability refers to the consistency of employment test scores over time and across measures. Validity refers to the accuracy of measurement. Validity can be assessed in terms of whether the measurement is based on a job specification (content validity), whether test scores correlate with performance criteria (predictive validity), and whether the test accurately measures what it purports to measure (construct validity).

2 Interviews are customarily used in conjunction with application forms, biographical information blanks, references, background investigations, medical examinations, cognitive ability tests, job knowledge tests, and work sample tests.

3 While the popularity of tests had declined somewhat with the passage of Equal Employment Opportunity (EEO) laws, in recent years there has been a dramatic resurgence of testing. The value of tests should not be overlooked since they are more objective than the interview and can provide a broader sampling of behavior. Cognitive ability tests are especially valuable for assessing verbal, quantitative, and reasoning abilities. Personality and interest tests are perhaps best for placement. Physical ability tests are most useful for predicting job performance, accidents, and injuries, particularly for demanding work. Job knowledge and work sample tests are achievement tests that are useful for determining if a candidate can perform the duties of the job without further training.

4 The employment interview is an important source of information about job applicants. The interview can be unstructured, wherein the interviewer is free to pursue whatever approach and sequence of topics might seem appropriate. Alternatively, an interview can be structured, wherein each applicant receives the same set of questions, which have preestablished answers. Some interviews are situational and questions can focus on hypothetical situations or actual behavioral descriptions of previous work experiences. Interviews can be conducted by a single individual, a panel, or via a computer interface. Regardless of the technique chosen, those who conduct interviews should receive special training to acquaint them with interviewing methods and Equal Employment Opportunities (EEO) considerations. The training should also make them more aware of the major findings from research studies on the interview and how they can apply these findings.

5 In the process of making decisions, all "can-do" and "will-do" factors should be assembled and weighted systematically so that the final decision can be based on a composite of the most reliable and valid information. While the clinical approach to decision-making is used more than the statistical approach, the former lacks the accuracy of the latter. Compensatory models allow a candidate's high score on one predictor to make up for a low score on another. However, multiple cutoffs and multiple hurdle approaches require minimal competency on each selection criterion. Whichever of these approaches is used, the goal is to select a greater proportion of individuals who will be successful on the job.

REVIEW QUESTIONS

Multiple Choice

Choose the letter of the word or phrase that best completes each statement.

1   _____   1. The process of choosing individuals who have revelant qualifications to fill existing jobs or projected job openings is known as
a. job fit.
b. job analysis.
c. selection.
d. recruiting.

1   _____   2. The selection procedure is generally the responsibility of the Human Resources (HR) Department however; the final decision about hiring a person in their department is made by
a. operating employees.
b. line managers.
c. staff managers.
d. management consultants.

1   _____   3. The extent to which two or more selection methods (interviews and tests, for example) yield similar results or are consistent is referred to as
a. reliability.
b. content validity.
c. predictive validity.
d. concurrent validity.

4. Performance on a test when compared with actual production records and other measures that are appropriate to each type of job is an example of
   a. cross-functional validity.
   b. internal reliability.
   c. compensatory models.
   d. criterion-related validity.

5. The two types of criterion-related validity are
   a. concurrent and predictive.
   b. content and internal reliability.
   c. predictive and cross-validity.
   d. face and construct validity.

6. Where it is not feasible to use the criterion-related approach, often because of limited samples of individuals, the method used is
   a. faith validity.
   b. reliability.
   c. construct validity.
   d. content validity.

7. This act gave students and their parents the right to inspect student personnel files. University administrators and faculty have been reluctant to provide anything other than general and often meaningless positive statements about student performance since the enactment of the
   a. Fair Labor Standard Act of 1938.
   b. Equal Pay Act of 1963.
   c. Age Discrimination and Employment Act of 1967.
   d. Family Educational Rights Privacy Act of 1974.

8. A device that measures the changes in breathing, blood pressure, and pulse of a person who is being questioned is a(n)
   a. polygraph test.
   b. assessment center test.
   c. achievement test.
   d. personality test.

9. One of the later steps in the selection process, because of its cost, is the
   a. interview.
   b. background investigation.
   c. employment test.
   d. medical examination.

10. The normal method of drug testing used by employers is
    a. biographical test.
    b. personality test.
    c. urine sampling.
    d. hair follicle test.

11. An objective and standardized measure of a sample of behavior that is used to gauge a person's knowledge, skills, abilities, and other characteristics is a(n)
    a. application form.
    b. physical exam.
    c. background investigation.
    d. employment test.

12. The type of employment test that measures a person's capacity to learn or acquire skills is a(n)
    a. aptitude test.
    b. work sample.
    c. assessment center.
    d. achievement tests.

13. The instrument that measures mental capabilities such as general intelligence, verbal fluency, numerical ability, and reasoning ability is
    a. personality tests.
    b. achievement tests.
    c. cognitive ability tests.
    d. assessment centers.

14. The type of instrument that measures disposition characteristics such as extroversion, agreeableness, conscientiousness, emotional stability, and openness to experience is a(n)
    a. achievement test.
    b. personality test.
    c. aptitude test.
    d. work sample test.

15. The mainstay of employment selection is the interview because of the following **EXCEPT FOR**
    a. small number of applicants.
    b. interviewer judgement.
    c. internal bias.
    d. good public relations.

_____ 16. The type of interview that the interviewer carefully refrains from influencing the applicant's remarks and the applicant is allowed the maximum amount of freedom in determining the course of the discussion is the
   a. nondirective interview.
   b. structured interview.
   c. situational interview.
   d. stress interview.

_____ 17. The type of interview that has a set of standardized questions (based on job analysis) and an established set of answers against which applicant responses can be rated and provides a more consistent basis for evaluating job candidates is the
   a. situational interview.
   b. nondirective interview.
   c. structured interview.
   d. assessment center.

_____ 18. The interviewing technique where the applicant is given a hypothetical incident and asked how he or she would respond is known as
   a. nondirective interview.
   b. situational interview.
   c. structured guide interview.
   d. work sample interview.

_____ 19. A selection technique where a board of recruiters is attempting to poll a candidate is
   a. situational interview.
   b. behavioral interview.
   c. structured guide interview.
   d. panel interview.

_____ 20. While all of the steps in the selection process are important, the most critical step is the decision to
   a. accept or reject applicants.
   b. utilize employment tests.
   c. use application forms.
   d. administer reference checks.

_____ 21. An evaluation of candidates on the basis of assembled information should focus on the factors of
   a. skills and aptitude analysis.
   b. can-do and will-do candidate analysis.
   c. achievement and potential analysis.
   d. job analysis and position descriptions.

5 _____ 22. The approach where those making the selection decision review
all the data on applicants before making the candidate choice is
the
a. statistical approach.
b. biographical approach.
c. clinical approach.
d. work sample analysis.

5 _____ 23. The selection decision that requires an applicant to achieve some
level of proficiency on all selection dimensions is
a. job analysis.
b. job specification.
c. multiple cutoff model.
d. job description.

5 _____ 24. The number of applicants compared with the number of persons
to be hired is called
a. selection ratio.
b. panel interview.
c. situational interview.
d. job description.

5 _____ 25. After a preliminary selection has been made in the employment
department, those applicants who appear to be most promising
are then referred to departments having vacancies; there they are
interviewed by the department managers, who usually make the
a. contract offer.
b. final hiring decision.
c. performance evaluation.
d. training criteria.

True/False

Identify the following statements as True or False.

1 _____ 1. In a person-organization fit, managers will pass up potential
employees if they don't embrace the values of the organization.

1 _____ 2. In most organizations, selection is an ongoing process for the
human resources specialist.

1 _____ 3. A selection procedure never should be validated before it is used.

objective 1

_____ 4. Research has proven that validity coefficients can often be generalized across situations.

objective 1

_____ 5. The closer the content of the selection instrument is to actual work samples or behaviors, the greater its content validity.

objective 1

_____ 6. The extent, to which a selection tool measures a theoretical construct, or trait, is known as construct validity.

objective 2

_____ 7. Most organizations require application forms to be completed because they provide a fairly quick and systematic means of obtaining a variety of information about the applicant.

objective 2

_____ 8. The only purpose of an application form is to provide information for deciding whether an applicant meets the minimum requirements of the job being offered.

objective 2

_____ 9. Both the biographical information blanks (BIB) and the application form can be scored like tests, and because biographical questions rarely have obviously right or wrong answers, BIBs are difficult to fake.

objective 2

_____ 10. Reference checking is commonly used to screen and select applicants and has always been successful in predicting employee performance.

objective 2

_____ 11. Graphology refers to a variety of systems of handwriting analysis, however it is never used by employers to make employment decisions.

objective 3

_____ 12. The number of U.S. companies that test employment candidates for drug use has decreased significantly.

objective 3

_____ 13. In the past decade, there has been a dramatic resurgence in the use of employment testing.

objective 3

_____ 14. Achievement tests require the applicant to perform tasks that are actually a part of the work required on the job.

objective 3

_____ 15. Despite their potential value, physical ability tests tend to work to the disadvantage of women and disabled job applicants.

objective 4

_____ 16. In using the nondirective interview approach, the interviewer listens carefully and does not argue, interrupt, or change the subject abruptly with the candidate.

4 objective _____ 17. A structured interview is more likely to provide the type of information needed for making sound decisions, however it increases the likelihood of legal charges of unfair discrimination.

4 objective _____ 18. A behavioral description interview focuses on actual work incidents in the interviewee's past, and inquires what the job applicant has done in a given job situation.

4 objective _____ 19. The panel interview is a situation consisting of three to five recruiters interviewing a group of potential employees at the same time.

5 objective _____ 20. Video interviews have several potential advantages related to flexibility, speed, and cost.

5 objective _____ 21. The decision strategy for selecting managerial and executive personnel will differ from the strategy used in selecting clerical and technical personnel.

5 objective _____ 22. In the statistical approach to decision-making, those making the selection decision review all the data on applicants.

5 objective _____ 23. The clinical approach to decision-making involves identifying the most valid predictors and weighting them through clinical methods such as multiple regression analysis.

5 objective _____ 24. The statistical approach of employment decision includes compensatory, multiple cutoff, and multiple hurdle models.

5 objective _____ 25. In large organizations, notifying applicants of the decision and making job offers is the responsibility of the employee.

Matching

Match each term with the proper definition.

Terms

a. achievement tests
b. aptitude tests
c. behavioral description interview (BDI)
d. compensatory model
e. concurrent validity
f. construct validity
g. content validity
h. criterion-related validity
i. cross-validation
j. multiple cutoff model
k. multiple hurdle model

l. nondirective interview
m. panel interview
n. predictive validity
o. reliability
p. selection
q. selection ratio
r. situational interview
s. structured interview
t. validity
u. validity generalization

Definitions

_____1. the process of choosing individuals who have relevant qualifications to fill existing or projected job openings

_____2. an interview in which an applicant is asked about what he or she actually did in a given situation

_____3. the extent to which applicants' test scores match criterion data obtained from those applicants/employees after they have been on the job for some indefinite period

_____4. an interview in which the applicant is allowed the maximum amount of freedom in determining the course of the discussion, while the interviewer carefully refrains from influencing the applicant's remarks

_____5. measures of what a person knows or can do right now

_____6. the extent to which test scores (or other predictor information) match criterion data obtained at about the same time from current employees

_____7. a sequential strategy in which only applicants with the highest scores at an initial test stage goes on to subsequent stages

_____8. the degree to which interviews, tests, and other selection procedures yield comparable data over time and alternative measures

_____9. measures of a person's capacity to learn or acquire skills

_____10. the extent to which validity coefficients can be generalized across
              situations

_____11. the extent to which a selection instrument, such as a test, adequately
              samples the knowledge and skills needed to perform a particular job

_____12. an interview in which an applicant is given a hypothetical incident and
              asked how he or she would respond to it

_____13. degree to which a test or selection procedure measures a person's
              attributes

_____14. verifying the results obtained from a validation study by administering a
              test or test battery to a different sample (drawn from the same population)

_____15. an interview in which a board of interviewers questions and observes a
              single candidate

_____16. selection decision model in which a high score in one area can make up
              for a low score in another area

_____17. the number of applicants compared with the number of persons hired

_____18. the extent to which a selection tool predicts, or significantly correlates,
              with important elements of work behavior

_____19. selection decision model that requires an applicant to achieve some
              minimum level of proficiency on all selection dimensions

_____20. an interview in which a set of standardized questions with an established
              set of answers is used

_____21. the extent to which a selection tool measures a theoretical construct or
              trait

Applications

1. The Bennett Mechanical Comprehension Test consists of a wide variety of tasks that measure the
   a. predictive validation test scores.
   b. concurrent validity of work samples.
   c. internal reliability of the interview.
   d. construct of mechanical comprehension.

2. Payless Shoe Source, based in Topeka, Kansas, has used a paper-and-pencil honesty employment test to reduce
   a. physical exams.
   b. employee theft.
   c. reference checks.
   d. background investigations.

3. Wal-Mart recently paid $6 million to settle a lawsuit involving
   a. Human Resources decision over sexual harassment.
   b. the Americans with Disabilities Act claim over affirmative action.
   c. the Americans with Disabilities Act claim pertaining to their hiring questionnaire.
   d. human resources decision pertaining to employment testing.

4. Cigna Insurance and Pinkerton Security and Investigation Services have developed expert systems to gather information pertaining to
   a. employment turnover and theft.
   b. preliminary information and candidate comparisons.
   c. reference and background checks.
   d. physical and mental disorders.

5. Companies such as AT&T, Dell Computer, Shell Oil, and Nike are using videoconference technologies to
   a. evaluate job candidates.
   b. evaluate job descriptions.
   c. analyze affirmative action.
   d. review job specifications.

How To Effectively Write a Resume and Successful Preparation for an Interview

1. The student should understand the guidelines for an effective resume. These guidelines should include:
   - Personal identification information, such as your name, address, telephone number, and email address.
   - Resume objectives. In other words, what are you looking for in terms of a job? It should relate in terms of career goals.
   - Education. This should be directly correlated with your objectives, and how can this be supported. This information should include courses taken as well as specific skills developed through these courses, such as computer skills, problem-solving skills, and communication skills.
   - Work experience. This information should relate to the occupational field in which one has worked. Make sure this supports that one is able to hold a job over a period of time. Transferable skills should be highlighted in regards to leadership, conflict resolution, time management, and stress management activities.
   - Awards, activities, and/or military experience. This should include community experience, voluntarism (food banks, scouting programs, etc.), and/or professional memberships, such as Rotary, Kiwanis, Lions, etc.

2. When developing a competitive advantage in preparation for an interview, a student is encouraged to perform the following tasks:
   - Research the firm. The library and/or Chamber of Commerce are an excellent source of information pertaining to a local business enterprise. Two specific sources are the *Wall Street Journal's* "Index to Businesses" and *Standard and Poors* "Industry Surveys".
   - Complete application forms. This should include proper English usage and spelling. Make sure to answer all application questions at the appropriate level of detail.
   - Prepare for interview. Anticipate questions pertaining to one's level of education, work experience, and awards and activities. Have questions for the recruiter following the interview. Questions such as, how soon do you plan to fill this position, growth opportunities, career development programs, orientation, training, etc.
   - Reference and background investigations. It is important for a student to ask for permission before using any individual's name for a reference.

SOLUTIONS

Multiple Choice:	True/False:	Matching:
1. c	1. True	1. p
2. b	2. True	2. c
3. a	3. False	3. n
4. d	4. True	4. l
5. a	5. True	5. a
6. d	6. True	6. e
7. d	7. True	7. k
8. a	8. False	8. o
9. d	9. True	9. b
10. c	10. False	10. u
11. d	11. False	11. g
12. a	12. False	12. r
13. c	13. True	13. t
14. b	14. False	14. i
15. c	15. True	15. m
16. a	16. True	16. d
17. c	17. False	17. q
18. b	18. True	18. h
19. d	19. False	19. j
20. a	20. True	20. s
21. b	21. True	21. f
22. c	22. False	
23. c	23. False	
24. a	24. True	
25. b	25. False	

False Statements from True/False

3.   A selection procedure **should be** validated before it is used.
8.   **One of the several purposes** of an application form is to provide information for deciding whether an applicant meets the minimum requirements of the job being offered.
10. Reference checking is commonly used to screen and select applicants **but has not proven successful** in predicting employee performance.
11. Graphology refers to a variety of systems of handwriting analysis **and is used by some** employers to make employment decisions.
12. The number of U.S. companies that test employment candidates for drug use has **increased** significantly.
14. Achievement tests **measure what a person knows or can do right now**.
17. A structured interview is more likely to provide the type of information needed for making sound decisions**; it also reduces the possibility** of legal charges of unfair discrimination.

19. The panel interview is a situation consisting of three to five recruiters interviewing a **single candidate** at the same time.
22. In the **clinical** approach to decision-making, those making the selection decision review all the data on applicants.
23. The **statistical** approach to decision-making involves identifying the most valid predictors and weighting them through **statistical** methods such as multiple regression analysis.
25. In large organizations, notifying applicants of the decision and making job offers is the responsibility of the **human resources department**.

Application

1. d
2. b
3. c
4. b
5. a

CHAPTER 6

TRAINING AND DEVELOPMENT

The student will learn the systems approach to training and development and be able to describe the components of training-needs assessment. You will be able to identify the principles of learning and how they facilitate training. In this chapter you will learn the types of training methods used for managers and non-managers. You will be able to discuss the advantages and disadvantages of various evaluation criteria. Finally, you will learn the special training programs that are currently popular.

LEARNING OBJECTIVES

After studying this chapter you should be able to

 Discuss the systems approach to training and development.

 Describe the components of training-needs assessment.

 Identify the principles of learning and describe how they facilitate training.

 Identify the types of training methods used for managers and non-managers.

 Discuss the advantages and disadvantages of various evaluation criteria.

 Describe the special training programs that are currently popular.

CHAPTER SUMMARY RELATING TO LEARNING OBJECTIVES

1 Today we find that organizational operations cover a broad range of subjects and involve personnel at all levels, from orientation through management development. In addition to providing the training needed for effective job performance, employers offer training in such areas as personal growth and wellness. In order to have effective training programs the systems approach is recommended. This approach consists of four phases: (1) needs assessment, (2) program design, (3) implementation, and (4) evaluation.

2 Needs assessment begins with organization analysis. Managers must establish a context for training by deciding where training is needed, how it connects with strategic goals, and how organizational resources can best be used. Task analysis is used to identify the knowledge, skills, and abilities that are needed by employees. Person analysis is used to identify which individuals need training.

3 In designing a training program, managers must consider the two fundamental preconditions for learning: readiness and motivation. In addition, principles of learning should be considered in order to create an environment that is conducive to learning. These principles include goal setting, meaningfulness, modeling, individual differences, active practice, whole-versus-part learning, distributed learning, feedback, and rewards and reinforcement.

4 In the training of non-managerial personnel, a wide variety of methods are available. On-the-job training is one of the most commonly used methods because it provides the advantage of hands-on experience and an opportunity to build a relationship between supervisor and employee. Apprenticeship training and internships are especially effective because they provide both on- and off-the-job experiences. Other off-the-job methods include the conference or discussion method, classroom training, programmed instruction, computer-based training, simulation, closed-circuit TV, teletraining, and interactive videodisc are all different training methods. All of these methods can make a contribution to the training effort with relatively little cost vis-à-vis the number of trainees who can be accommodated.

The training and development of managers is a multibillion-dollar business. As with non-managerial personnel, a wide variety of training methods are used for developing managers. On-the-job experiences include coaching, understudy assignment, job rotation, lateral transfer, project and committee assignments, and staff meetings. Off-the-job experiences include analysis of case studies, management games, role-playing, and behavior modeling.

5 Evaluation of a training program should focus on several criteria: participant reactions, learning, behavior change on the job, and bottom-line results. Transfer of training is measured via examination of the degree to which trained skills are demonstrated back on the job. Benchmarking and utility analysis help evaluate the impact of training and provide the information for further needs assessment.

6 Special issues in training involve those programs that are important to a broad range of employees. Orientation training, for example, begins and continues throughout an employee's service with an organization. By participating in a formal orientation program, employees acquire the knowledge, skills, and attitudes that increase the probabilities of their success with the organization. To make an orientation effective there should be close cooperation between the Human Resources department and other departments in all phases of the program, from initial planning through follow-up and evaluation. Basic skills training, team training, sensitivity training, and diversity training are also critically important in today's organizations.

REVIEW QUESTIONS

Multiple Choice

Choose the letter of the word or phrase that best completes each statement.

1 _____ 1. The process most often used to describe almost any effort initiated by an organization to foster learning among its members is
   a. orientation.
   b. training.
   c. performance appraisal.
   d. job evaluation.

1 _____ 2. The primary objective of training is to contribute to the organization's
   a. overall goals.
   b. cultural diversity.
   c. corporate downsizing.
   d. job sharing.

2 _____ 3. The examination of the environment, strategies, and resources of the organization to determine where training emphasis should be placed is
   a. management by objectives.
   b. critical incident.
   c. organization analysis.
   d. job ranking.

4. Reviewing the job description and specifications to identify the activities needed to perform a particular job and the knowledge, skills, and aptitude needed to perform them involves
   a. personality enhancement.
   b. socialization process.
   c. behavior modification.
   d. task analysis.

5. The process in determining which individual employees need training and who does not is
   a. person analysis.
   b. job evaluation.
   c. job analysis.
   d. employee orientation.

6. The success of a firm's training program is dependent upon
   a. employee orientation.
   b. performance appraisal.
   c. job analysis.
   d. training design.

7. As a result of conducting organization task and person analysis, managers will have a more complete picture of the training needs, when they can state the desired outcomes of training through written
   a. employee contracts.
   b. job specifications.
   c. instructional objectives.
   d. implied contracts.

8. Two preconditions for learning affecting the success of those who are to receive training are
   a. readiness and motivation.
   b. task identity and task significance.
   c. behavior and personality.
   d. culture and socialization process.

9. Trainees will learn faster and have longer retention when there training is spaced out over shorter periods of time. This type of training is
   a. distributed learning.
   b. feedback training.
   c. active practice learning.
   d. passive repetitive learning.

10. As an employee's training progresses, feedback serves two related purposes, which are
    a. employee probation and career development.
    b. knowledge of results and employee motivation.
    c. job security and job protection.
    d. employee results and performance evaluation.

11. Training that provides both hands-on experience under normal working conditions and opportunities for the trainer, manager, or senior employee to build good relationships with new employees is called
    a. cooperative training.
    b. on-the-job training.
    c. competency assessment.
    d. behavior modification.

12. The type of training program that requires cooperation between organizations and their labor unions, between industry and government, or between organizations and local school systems are
    a. work seminars.
    b. career development programs.
    c. job rotation activities.
    d. apprenticeship programs.

13. The type of training that provides practical on-the-job experience with formal classes is known as
    a. on-the-job training.
    b. vestibule training.
    c. job instruction training.
    d. cooperative training.

14. A program that is jointly sponsored by colleges, universities, and a variety of organizations, offer students the chance to get real-world experience while finding out how they will perform in work organizations is a(n)
    a. coaching technique.
    b. mentor.
    c. performance evaluation.
    d. internship program.

_____ 15. Training that is particularly effective in allowing individual trainees to work at their own pace is called
  a. on-the-job training.
  b. programmed instruction.
  c. apprenticeship training.
  d. cooperative training.

_____ 16. The use of artificial intelligence and hypermedia to provide just the help a performer needs to do a job, just when the performance needs it, and in just the form in which he or she needs it is known as
  a. performance support systems.
  b. computer-assisted training.
  c. coaching.
  d. job training.

_____ 17. A training method that emphasizes realism in equipment and its operation at minimum cost and maximum safety is known as a(n)
  a. internship program.
  b. on-the-job training program.
  c. work sampling method.
  d. simulation method.

_____ 18. Assuming the attitudes and behavior of others involved in a particular problem is known as
  a. job instruction training.
  b. role playing.
  c. orientation.
  d. anxiety training.

_____ 19. The following basic criteria are available to evaluate training programs **EXCEPT FOR**
  a. learning.
  b. predictions.
  c. behavior.
  d. results.

_____ 20. One of the simplest and most common approaches to training evaluation is assessing
  a. employee needs.
  b. leadership styles.
  c. coaching techniques.
  d. participant reactions.

_____ 21. A systems model of training involves the following processes, **EXCEPT FOR**
a. needs assessment.
b. principles of learning.
c. position descriptions.
d. evaluation.

_____ 22. The formal process of familiarizing new employees with the organization, their jobs, and their work unit is
a. team training.
b. diversity training.
c. sensitivity training.
d. orientation training.

_____ 23. Essential occupational qualifications, having profound implications for product quality, customer service, internal efficiency, and workplace and environmental safety is known as
a. job instruction training.
b. basic skills training.
c. on-the-job training.
d. coaching and mentoring.

_____ 24. An awareness of the varied demographics of the workforce, the challenges of affirmative action, the dynamics of stereotyping, the changing values of the workforce, and the potential competitive payoffs from bringing different people together for a common purpose is known as
a. diversity training.
b. basic skills training.
c. on-the-job training.
d. computer-assisted training.

_____ 25. To avoid the pitfalls of substandard diversity training, managers will want to do the following **EXCEPT FOR**
a. forge a strategic link.
b. check out consultant qualifications.
c. analyze and review performance appraisal methods.
d. choose training methods carefully.

True/False

Identify the following statements as True or False.

1 _____ 1. As a result of training, employees may be even more ineffective on the job and will not be able to perform other jobs in other areas or at higher levels.

1 _____ 2. The training program of the systems approach involves three phases: needs assessment, program design, and implementation.

1 _____ 3. The last step in needs assessment is identifying the broad forces that can influence training needs.

2 _____ 4. Task analysis involves reviewing the job description and specification to identify the activities performed in a particular job and the knowledge, skills, and aptitudes (KSAs) needed to perform them.

2 _____ 5. Person analysis involves determining which employees require training and, equally important, which do not.

2 _____ 6. Most employees are motivated by certain common needs, and they are similar in the relative importance of these needs at any given time.

3 _____ 7. The value of goal setting for focusing and motivating behavior extends into training.

3 _____ 8. Even modeling the wrong behavior can be helpful if it shows trainees what not to do and the appropriate behavior is then demonstrated.

3 _____ 9. Feedback is simply the feeling of accomplishment that follows successful performance of training.

4 _____ 10. The success of any training effort will depend in large part on the teaching skills and personal characteristics of those responsible for conducting the training.

4 _____ 11. All types of organizations use on-the-job training (OJT) and it is one of the most efficiently implemented training methods.

4 _____ 12. With apprenticeship training, thorough instruction and experience, both on and off the job, in the practical and theoretical aspects of the work are given to individuals entering the industry.

13. The term "cooperative training" is typically used in connection with high school and college programs that incorporate part-time or full-time experiences.

14. The programmed training method lends itself particularly to training in areas where information can be presented in lectures, demonstrations, films, and videotapes or through computer instruction.

15. While programmed instruction increases the amount an individual learns, it typically decreases the speed at which he or she learns.

16. By presenting managers with the opportunities to perform under pressure and to learn from their mistakes, on-the-job development experiences are some of the most powerful and commonly used techniques.

17. Seminars and conferences, unlike classroom instruction, are useful for bringing groups of people together for training and development.

18. Testing knowledge and skills before beginning a training program gives a baseline standard on trainees that can be measured again after training to determine improvement.

19. Organizations with sophisticated training systems look to training to support short-term strategy and change, not to gain long-term financial returns from their investments.

20. To evaluate benchmarking standards, the late W. Edwards Deming's classic four-step process for needs assessment advocates that managers plan, do, check, and act.

21. To use benchmarking successfully in training, managers must clearly define the measures of competency and performance and must objectively assess the current situation and identify areas of improvement.

22. To get new employees off to a good start, organizations generally offer a formal orientation program.

23. The supervisor has the least important role in the orientation program.

_____ 24. While there are different possible approaches to ensuring that employees have basic skills, the establishment of in-house basic skills programs has decreased in favor.

_____ 25. Organizations that have been successful with diversity training realize that it is a long-term process that requires the highest level of skill.

Matching

Match each term with the proper definition.

Terms

a. apprenticeship training
b. behavior modeling
c. behavior modification
d. benchmarking
e. competency assessment
f. computer-assisted instruction (CAI)
g. computer-managed instruction (CMI)
h. cooperative training
i. distributed learning

j. instructional objectives
k. internship programs
l. on-the-job training (OJT)
m. organization analysis
n. orientation
o. person analysis
p. task analysis
q. transfer of training

Definitions

_____ 1. an examination of the environment, strategies, and resources of the organization to determine where training emphasis should be placed

_____ 2. programs jointly sponsored by colleges, universities, and other organizations that offer students the opportunity to gain real-life experience while allowing them to find out how they will perform in an organization

_____ 3. formal process of familiarizing new employees with the organization, their jobs, and their work units

_____ 4. training program that combines practical on-the-job experience with formal educational classes

_____ 5. effective application of principles to what is required on the job

_____   6. system of training in which a worker entering the skilled trades is given thorough instruction and experience, both on and off the job, in the practical and theoretical aspects of the work

_____   7. determines which employees require training and which do not

_____   8. a system normally employed in conjunction with CAI that uses a computer to generate and score tests and to determine level proficiency

_____   9. process of determining what the content of a training program should be on the basis of a study of the tasks or duties involved in the job

_____   10. desired outcomes of a training program

_____   11. approach that demonstrates desired behavior and gives trainees the chance to practice and role-play those behaviors and receive feedback

_____   12. method by which employees are given hands-on experience with instructions from their supervisor or other trainer

_____   13. system that delivers instructional material directly through a computer terminal in an interactive format

_____   14. process of measuring an organization's own services and practices against the recognized industry leaders in order to identify areas for improvement

_____   15. analysis of the sets of skills and knowledge needed for decision-oriented and knowledge-intensive jobs

_____   16. technique that operates on the principle that behavior that is rewarded or positively reinforced will be exhibited more frequently in the future, whereas behavior that is penalized or unrewarded will decrease in frequency

_____   17. spacing out the training in order to accomplish faster learning and longer retention

Applications

1. According to *Training Magazine*'s ongoing industry report, U.S. businesses spend nearly $60 billion each year on
   a. public relations.
   b. formal training.
   c. trade shows.
   d. workshops and seminars.

2. Based on a list of identified job tasks, KLM Royal Dutch Airlines trains cabin attendants in customer service through the use of
   a. job instruction training.
   b. vestibule training.
   c. on-the-job training.
   d. computer assisted training.

3. Arizona State University, Cornell University, and many other universities allow students to earn college credits on the basis of successful job performance and fulfillment of established program requirements. This type of training program is a(n)
   a. simulation method.
   b. internship program.
   c. cooperative training.
   d. behavior modeling program.

4. Instead of looking for immediate payback in their training programs, organizations such as Florida Power and Light, Motorola, and Hawker de Havilland views training in terms of its
   a. long term strategy and change.
   b. teleconferencing control.
   c. feedback application.
   d. preventive maintenance.

5. Lazarus Department stores was able to cut orientation-training time in half, orienting 2,500 new employees in six weeks, through the use of
   a. job analysis.
   b. job evaluation.
   c. computer-based training.
   d. performance appraisal.

How To Embark Upon Orientation and Training

1. How would you prepare, inquire about orientation and training programs? During the interview, a student should inquire about eh orientation and training they will receive once hired. To minimize anxiety, individuals should address the question of the orientation program offered to new hires. An orientation program should address the job description, the people, or employees you are expected to work with, and the cross over of working with inter-departments. A checklist is recommended to permit the new employee everything there is to know pertaining to the performance of the job. Questions should be addressed pertaining to the training programs offered to new employees. The objective of the training program: The type of training program, and the evaluation used of the training program. Also questions as to the length of the training program, how often individuals are retrained, and is retraining continuous with the organization.

2. As a student, how important is it to recognize how to benefit from an organization's orientation and training program? The benefits of an orientation program offered by a company should address the minimization of anxiety experienced by many new employees. A new recruit should work with the Human Resources Department and learn everything about the organization's policies, procedures, and rules. Inquire about an occupational manual to learn everything there is to know about the new job. A training program should be continuous and offered to new employees. Inquire about the training offered, how long does it last, and the type of training methods you will receive.

SOLUTIONS

Multiple Choice:	True/False:	Matching:
1. b	1. False	1. m
2. a	2. False	2. k
3. c	3. False	3. n
4. d	4. True	4. h
5. a	5. True	5. q
6. d	6. False	6. a
7. c	7. True	7. o
8. a	8. True	8. g
9. a	9. False	9. p
10. b	10. True	10. j
11. b	11. False	11. b
12. d	12. True	12. l
13. d	13. True	13. f
14. d	14. False	14. d
15. b	15. False	15. e
16. a	16. True	16. c
17. d	17. False	17. i
18. b	18. True	
19. b	19. False	
20. d	20. True	
21. c	21. True	
22. d	22. True	
23. b	23. False	
24. a	24. False	
25. c	25. True	

False Statements from True/False

1. As a result of training, employees may be even more **effective** on the job and **may** be able to perform other jobs in other areas or at higher levels.
2. The training program of the systems approach involves **four** phases: needs assessment, program design, implementation, **and evaluation**.
3. The **first** step in needs assessment is identifying the broad forces that can influence training needs.
6. **While** most employees are motivated by certain common needs, and they **differ from one another** in the relative importance of these needs at any given time.
9. **Reinforcement** is simply the feeling of accomplishment that follows successful performance of training.
11. All types of organizations use on-the-job training (OJT), **however** it is one of the most **poorly** implemented training methods.

14. The **classroom** training method lends itself particularly to training in areas where information can be presented in lectures, demonstrations, films, and videotapes or through computer instruction.

15. While programmed instruction **may not increase** the amount an individual learns, it typically **increases** the speed at which he or she learns.

17. Seminars and conferences, **like** classroom instruction, are useful for bringing groups of people together for training and development.

19. Organizations with sophisticated training systems look to training to support **long-term** strategy and change more than **short-term** financial returns from their investments.

23. The supervisor has the **most** important role in the orientation program.

24. While there are different possible approaches to ensuring that employees have basic skills, the establishment of in-house basic skills programs has **come increasingly into** favor.

Applications

1. b
2. c
3. b
4. a
5. c

CHAPTER 7

CAREER DEVELOPMENT

Career development programs are a fairly recent addition to the functions performed by human resources departments. These programs are designed to enable employees to match their needs for growth and development with those of the organization. Carefully organized job progressions are established so employees may plan a lifetime career with the organization. In developing these programs special efforts have been made to provide opportunities for managers, women, and minorities. Through workshops and counseling, employee strengths and needs are identified and career paths are selected. Employers can also facilitate the career development of members of minority groups and of dual-career couples.

LEARNING OBJECTIVES

After studying this chapter you should be able to:

 Explain how a career development program integrates individual and organizational needs.

 Describe the conditions that help to make a career development program successful.

 Discuss how job opportunities can be inventoried and employee potential assessed.

 Describe the methods used for identifying and developing managerial talent.

 Cite the ways in which employers can facilitate the career development of women.

 Cite the ways in which employers can facilitate the career development of members of minority groups and of dual-career couples.

Describe the various aspects of personal career development that one should consider.

CHAPTER SUMMARY RELATING TO LEARNING OBJECTIVES

1 A career development program is a dynamic process that should integrate individual employee needs with those of the organization. It is the responsibility of the employee to identify his or her own knowledge, skills, and aptitudes as well as interests and values and to seek out information about career options. The organization should provide information about its mission, policies, plans and what it will provide in the way of training and development for the employee.

2 In order to be successful, a career development program must receive the support of top management. The program should reflect the goals and the culture of the organization. Managerial personnel at all levels must be trained in the fundamentals of job design, performance appraisal, career planning, and counseling. Employees should have an awareness of the organization's philosophy and its goals; otherwise they will not know how their goals match those of the organization. Human resources management policies, especially those concerning rotation, transfers, and promotions, should be consistent with the goals. The objectives and opportunities of the career development program should be announced widely throughout the organization.

3 Job opportunities may be identified by studying jobs and determining the knowledge and skills each one requires. Once that is accomplished, it is possible to plan job progressions. These progressions can then serve as a basis for developing career paths. Once career paths are developed and employees are identified on the career ladders, it is possible to inventory the jobs and determine where individuals with the required skills and knowledge are needed or will be needed.

4 Identifying and developing managerial talent is a responsibility of all managers. In addition to immediate superiors, there should be others in the organization who can nominate and sponsor employees with promise. Many organizations use assessment centers to identify managerial talent and recommend developmental experiences in order that each individual may reach her or his full potential. Mentoring has been found to be valuable for providing guidance and support to potential managers.

5 The first step in facilitating the career development of women is to eliminate barriers to advancement. The formation of women's networks, the providing of special training for women, the acceptance of women as valued members of the organization, the providing of mentors for women, and accommodating families have been found to be effective ways to facilitate a woman's career development.

6 While a diversified workforce is composed of many different groups, an important segment is minority groups. In addition to creating conditions that are favorable for recognizing and rewarding performance, many organizations have special programs such as internships that provide hands-on experience as well as special training opportunities. Another group that requires the attention of management is composed of dual-career couples who often need to have flexible working schedules.

7 In choosing a career, one should use all available resources. Consideration should be given to internal factors such as academic aptitude and achievement, occupational aptitudes and skills, communication skills, leadership abilities, and interests and values. External factors such as economic conditions, employment trends, and job market information must also be considered. Use of skill and interest inventories should be utilized to assist one to choose a career. Utilizing various publications, including those published by the government should assess long-term employment opportunities in an occupational field. Keeping a career in perspective so as to have a balanced life is desirable. While work is usually a primary factor in overall quality of life, one should give proper attention to physical health, harmonious family and interpersonal relationships, and interests and activities outside of one's career.

REVIEW QUESTIONS

Multiple Choice

Choose the letter of the word or phrase that best completes each statement.

1 _____   1. A common approach to establishing a career development program is to integrate it with the existing
a. HR functions and structures in the organization.
b. marketing and production plant.
c. labor and employment contract.
d. implicit and explicit contract.

2 _____   2. A career development program should be viewed as a dynamic process that matches the needs of the organization with the needs of
a. customers.
b. business agents.
c. employees.
d. competition.

3. If career development is to succeed, it must receive the complete support of
   a. business agents.
   b. management consultants.
   c. labor unions.
   d. top management.

4. Know-how competency is broken down into the following types of job knowledge **EXCEPT FOR**
   a. featherbedding.
   b. technical.
   c. managerial.
   d. human relations.

5. The principal criteria for determining promotions for an employee are
   a. experience, mental agility and physical well being.
   b. intuition, judgment, stability.
   c. character, capacity, learning ability.
   d. merit, seniority, and potential.

6. Individuals who look forward to change or want a chance to learn more may seek out
   a. complacency.
   b. compassion of job duties.
   c. to transfer to a new job.
   d. featherbedding or job enlargement.

7. The following require individuals to adjust to new job demands and usually to a different work environment **EXCEPT FOR**
   a. demotions.
   b. promotions.
   c. transfers.
   d. production bottlenecks.

8. Given limited career opportunities within firms, coupled with the need for talent in other companies, many individuals are discovering that their best career options may involve
   a. promotion.
   b. organizational exit.
   c. labor contracts.
   d. vertical movement.

3   _____   9. Services that can be used to enhance a productive employee's career, as well as to terminate an employee who is unproductive are
a. assessment centers.
b. outplacement services.
c. in-basket methods of training.
d. mentoring methods.

4   _____   10. Under the boundaryless career model, success depends on the following **EXCEPT FOR**
a. continually learning new skills.
b. demotion.
c. developing new relationships.
d. capitalizing on existing skills and relationships.

4   _____   11. The concept that directs attention to the developmental needs of employees, both in their present jobs and in managerial jobs to which they may be promoted, is a(n)
a. mentoring function.
b. dual-career track.
c. inventory of managerial positions.
d. relocation service.

4   _____   12. One of the most valuable methods for evaluating personnel is a(n)
a. assessment center.
b. job transfer.
c. dual-career track.
d. content plateau.

4   _____   13. As employees approach retirement, they may be encouraged to participate in
a. labor unions.
b. team development.
c. participative management.
d. preretirement programs.

5   _____   14. To combat difficulty in advancing to management positions, women have developed their own
a. assessment centers.
b. women's networks.
c. labor unions.
d. structural plateaus.

5 _____ 15. Many employers now offer special training to women who are
a. in a glass ceiling career.
b. on a career plateau.
c. in an outplacement program.
d. on a management career path.

5 _____ 16. One of the major problems that women have faced is that of having both a
a. managerial career and family.
b. career path and plateau.
c. dual-career marriage and fast-tracking program.
d. mentoring function and relocation services.

6 _____ 17. One way for a college student to learn on the job and gain hands-on experience is through a(n)
a. assessment center.
b. fast-tracking program.
c. job specification.
d. internship program.

6 _____ 18. Flexible working schedules are the most frequent organizational accommodation to
a. dual-career couples.
b. single households.
c. assembly-line workers.
d. professional employees.

6 _____ 19. The main problem dual-career couples face is the threat of
a. promotion.
b. dual incomes.
c. relocation.
d. job enlargement.

7 _____ 20. The stages of career development include the following **EXCEPT FOR**
a. organizational entry.
b. protean career.
c. late career.
d. preparation for work.

7 _____ 21. To succeed as a manager, one must achieve a high level of proficiency in the following areas **EXCEPT FOR**
a. communication.
b. time management.
c. assertiveness training.
d. interpersonal relationships.

22. The old model of "the organization man" who starts and stays with the same company is being replaced by a more flexible career model that Hall calls a
    a. organization dynamic.
    b. protean career.
    c. adjournment stage.
    d. structural plateau.

23. An employee whose promotions have leveled off and who will now have to leave the organization to find new opportunities and challenges is at the
    a. content plateau.
    b. structural plateau.
    c. life plateau.
    d. career plateau.

24. When a person has learned a job too well and is bored with day-to-day activities, they have reached a
    a. content plateau.
    b. career plateau.
    c. life plateau.
    d. structural plateau.

25. Individual entrepreneurs who consider starting a small business can obtain assistance from the
    a. local tax bureau.
    b. Small Business Administration (SBA).
    c. retail credit bureau.
    d. Equal Employment Opportunity Commission.

True/False

Identify the following statements as True or False.

1. Managers should take responsibility for their employees' careers, offering continuing assistance and providing information about the organization, job and career opportunities available.

2. Significant career growth can occur when individual initiative combines with organizational opportunity.

3. For a program to be effective, managerial personnel at all levels must be trained in the fundamentals of job design, performance appraisal, career planning, and counseling.

objective 2 _____ 4. Dealing with uncertainty is the most minor challenge an individual faces in his or her career.

objective 2 _____ 5. Individuals engaged in meaningful career planning should be aware of exit interviews of past employers.

objective 3 _____ 6. Unlike individuals, organizations rarely change their directions or adjust their strategies to cope with change.

objective 3 _____ 7. While most organizations should never concentrate on developing job progressions for managerial, professional, and technical jobs, progressions can be developed for some categories of jobs.

objective 3 _____ 8. Transfers make it possible for an organization to place its employees in jobs where there is a greater need for their services and where they can acquire new knowledge and skills.

objective 4 _____ 9. Individuals pursuing boundaryless careers may develop a portfolio of employment opportunities by proactively moving from employer to employer.

objective 4 _____ 10. Identifying and developing talent in individuals is a role that all managers should take lightly.

objective 4 _____ 11. Only immediate managers should have the power to evaluate, nominate, and sponsor employees with promise.

objective 4 _____ 12. Assessment centers have proved quite valuable in identifying managerial talent and in helping with the development of individuals, however they tend to favor those who are strong in interpersonal skills and have the ability to influence others.

objective 4 _____ 13. A career-planning workshop offers experience similar to those provided by workbooks with the advantage of providing a chance to compare and discuss attitudes, concerns, and plans with others in similar situations.

objective 5 _____ 14. Organizations are no longer concerned with increasing the proportion of women they employ as managers.

objective 5 _____ 15. As a complement to mentoring, where relationships are more random, networking relationships tend to be more limited and permanent.

_____ 16. The advancement of women in management has been increased favorably by a series of sex-role stereotypes that have shaped the destiny of working women.

_____ 17. Opportunities for women to move into management positions are definitely improving.

_____ 18. The development of women managers demands a better understanding of women's needs and of the requirements of management.

_____ 19. The male black or Hispanic manager who aspires to higher levels in an organization is likely to find that although his career may start off well, he may encounter barriers as he reaches middle management making it very difficult to move to the top.

_____ 20. In recent years black females have been rising more rapidly than black males in corporate America.

_____ 21. More employees are willing to relocate without assistance for their spouses.

_____ 22. In career development as one matures, knowledge, skills, abilities, and attitudes as well as career aspirations change.

_____ 23. In career development, the retirement stage is a time when careful planning, based on sound information, should be the focus.

_____ 24. Unsuccessful career development depends in part on an individual's ability to conduct an accurate self-evaluation.

_____ 25. In keeping a career in perspective for most people, work is a primary factor in the overall quality of their lives.

Matching

Match each term with the proper definition.

Terms

a. assessment center
b. career counseling
c. career paths
d. career plateau
e. dual-career partnerships
f. entrepreneur
g. fast-track program
h. in-basket training

i. job progressions
j. leaderless group discussions
k. mentoring functions
l. mentors
m. outplacement services
n. promotion
o. relocation services
p. transfer

Definitions

_____ 1. executives who coach, advise, and encourage individuals of lesser rank

_____ 2. lines of advancement in an occupational field within an organization

_____ 3. services provided to an employee who is transferred to a new location, which might include help in moving, in selling a home, in orienting to a new culture, and/or in learning a new language

_____ 4. one who starts, organizes, manages, and assumes responsibility for a business or other enterprise

_____ 5. process by which individuals are evaluated as they participate in a series of situations that resemble what they might be called upon to handle on the job

_____ 6. situation in which for either organizational or personal reasons the probability of moving up the career ladder is low

_____ 7. placement of an individual in another job for which the duties, responsibilities, status, and remuneration are approximately equal to those of the previous job

_____ 8. hierarchy of jobs a new employee might experience, ranging from a starting job to jobs that successively require more knowledge and/or skill

_____ 9. change of assignment to a job at a higher level in the organization

_____ 10. program that encourages young managers with high potential to remain with an organization by enabling them to advance more rapidly than those with less potential

_____ 11. process of discussing with employees their current job activities and performance, their personal and career interests, their personal skills, and suitable career development objectives

_____ 12. services provided by organizations to help terminated employees find a new job

_____ 13. functions concerned with the career advancement and psychological aspects of the person being mentored

_____ 14. marriages in which both members follow their own careers and actively support each other's career development

_____ 15. assessment center process for evaluating trainees by simulating a real-life work situation

_____ 16. assessment center process that places trainees in a conference setting to discuss an assigned topic, either with or without designated group roles

Applications

_____ 1. Sears studies its jobs carefully and measures know-how, problem solving, and accountability in order to identify and assign weights to each job. This is an example of using
   a. performance appraisals.
   b. assessment centers.
   c. job competencies.
   d. job progressions.

_____ 2. Douglas Bray and his associates at AT&T evaluate individuals as they participate in a series of situations that resemble what they might be called upon to handle on the job. This process is a(n)
   a. career path.
   b. career plateau.
   c. mentoring function.
   d. assessment center.

4 _____ 3. The MS Foundation for Women provides an opportunity for girls 9 to 15 years to spend a day with mothers or friends on the job. This is a form of
   a. assessment center.
   b. mentoring.
   c. dual-career partnerships.
   d. fast-track program.

5 _____ 4. Paine Webber, Suntrust Bank, Quaker Oats Company, Corning, Inc., and Pacific Telesis have inaugurated programs that are mutually advantageous to the career-oriented woman by offering alternative career paths, extended leave, flextime, job sharing, and telecommuting. These organizations are
   a. encouraging job transfers.
   b. using assessment centers.
   c. accommodating families.
   d. promoting fast-track programs.

6 _____ 5. Inroads, Inc., offers qualified minority college students a package that includes tutoring, counseling, and an opportunity to learn on-the-job training and gain hands-on experience with large corporations. This organization is providing
   a. internships.
   b. career counseling.
   c. job progressions.
   d. fast-track programs.

How to Select and Develop a Career

In selecting a career a student is encouraged to take advantages of the services offered by your educational institution. Services should include personality test, interest inventory test, aptitude test, and achievement test. You should be encouraged to take advantage of these services, and understand your strength to project a positive image to a perspective employer.

After initial placement with an employer, you have the responsibility of inquiring about a career development program with your employer. The organization is responsible for supplying information about its mission, policies, and plans and for providing support for employee self-assessment, training, and development. Your employer may offer the following career development programs: Career Planning Workbooks, Career Planning Workshops, Career Counseling, Career Self-Management Training, or Mentoring.

SOLUTIONS

Multiple Choice:	**True/False:**	**Matching:**
1. a	1. False	1. l
2. c	2. True	2. c
3. d	3. True	3. o
4. a	4. False	4. f
5. d	5. False	5. a
6. c	6. False	6. d
7. d	7. False	7. p
8. b	8. True	8. i
9. b	9. True	9. n
10. b	10. False	10. g
11. c	11. False	11. b
12. a	12. True	12. m
13. d	13. True	13. k
14. b	14. False	14. e
15. d	15. False	15. h
16. a	16. False	16. j
17. d	17. True	
18. a	18. True	
19. c	19. True	
20. b	20. True	
21. c	21. False	
22. b	22. True	
23. b	23. False	
24. a	24. False	
25. b	25. True	

False Statements from True/False

1. Managers should **encourage employees to** take responsibility for their **own** careers, offering continuing assistance and providing information about the organization, job and career opportunities available.
4. Dealing with uncertainty is the **biggest challenge** an individual faces in his or her career.
5. Individuals engaged in meaningful career planning **must not only have an awareness of the organization's philosophy, but they must have a good understanding of the organization's more immediate goals**.
6. **Similar to** individuals, organizations **also** change their directions or adjust their strategies to cope with change.
7. While most organizations **should** concentrate on developing job progressions for managerial, professional, and technical jobs, progressions can be developed for **all** categories of jobs.

10. Identifying and developing talent in individuals is a role that all managers should take **seriously**.
11. **In addition to** immediate managers **there should be others in the organization who** have the power to evaluate, nominate, and sponsor employees with promise.
14. Organizations are **continually** concerned with increasing the proportion of women they employ as managers.
15. As a complement to mentoring, where relationships are more **selective**, networking relationships tend to be more **varied and temporary**.
16. The advancement of women in management has been **hindered** by a series of sex-role stereotypes that have shaped the destiny of working women.
21. **Fewer** employees are willing to relocate without assistance for their spouses.
23. In career development, the **preparation for work stage** is a time when careful planning, based on sound information, should be the focus.
24. **Successful** career development depends in part on an individual's ability to conduct an accurate self-evaluation.

Applications

1. c
2. d
3. b
4. c
5. a

CHAPTER 8

APPRAISING AND IMPROVING PERFORMANCE

A major function of human resources management is the appraisal and improvement of employee performance. In establishing a performance appraisal program, managers should give careful attention to its objectives and to the criteria against which employees are to be evaluated. Court decisions have emphasized the importance of having carefully defined and measurable criteria. Newer methods and techniques for appraisal are replacing some of the older methods that are more subject to errors. The methods used should be consistent with the objectives of appraisal in the particular organization. Through interviews, managers can give information from the appraisal to subordinates and make plans for improving performance.

LEARNING OBJECTIVES

After studying this chapter you should be able to

 Explain the purposes of performance appraisals and the reasons they can sometimes fail.

 Identify the characteristics of an effective appraisal program.

 Describe the different sources of appraisal information.

 Explain the various methods used for performance evaluation.

 Outline the characteristics of an effective performance appraisal interview.

CHAPTER SUMMARY RELATING TO LEARNING OBJECTIVES

1 Performance appraisal programs serve many purposes, but in general those purposes can be clustered into two categories: administrative and developmental. The administrative purposes include decisions about who will be promoted, transferred, or laid off. They can also include compensation decisions and the like. Developmental decisions include those related to improving and enhancing an individual's capabilities. These include identifying a person's strengths and weaknesses, eliminating external performance obstacles, establishing training needs, and so on. The combination of administrative and developmental purposes of performance appraisal reflect, in a specific way, human resources management's larger role of integrating the individual with the organization.

In many organizations, performance appraisals are seen as a necessary evil. Managers frequently avoid conducting appraisals because they dislike playing the role of judge. Further, if managers are not adequately trained, subjectivity and organizational politics can distort the reviews. This situation tends to be self-defeating in that such managers frequently do not develop good feedback skills and are often not prepared to conduct an appraisal. As a consequence, the appraisal is done begrudgingly once a year and then forgotten about.

2 The success of an organization depends largely on the performance of its human resources. To determine the contributions of each individual, it is necessary to have a formal appraisal program with clearly stated objectives. Carefully defined performance standards that are reliable, strategically relevant, and free from either criterion deficiency or contamination are essential foundations for evaluation. Appraisal systems must also comply with the law. Appraisals should be treated with the same concerns for validity as are selection tests. For example, ratings must be job-related, employees must understand their performance standards in advance, appraisers must be able to observe job performance, appraisers must be trained, feedback must be given, and an appeals procedure must be established.

3 Using multiple raters is frequently a good idea because different individuals see different facets of an employee's performance. The supervisor, for example, has legitimate authority over an employee and is in a good position to discern whether he or she is contributing to the goals of the organization. Peers and team members, on the other hand, often have an unfiltered view of an employee's work activity, particularly related to issues such as cooperation and dependability. Subordinates often provide good information about whether an employee is facilitating their work, and customers (both internal and external) can convey the extent to which an employee adds value and meets their requirements. Self-appraisal is useful, if for no other reason than it encourages employees to think about their strengths, weaknesses, and future goals. An increasing number of organizations are using multiple raters—or 360-degree appraisal—to get a more comprehensive picture of employee performance. Regardless of the source of appraisal information, appraisers should be thoroughly trained in the particular methods they will use in evaluating their subordinates. Participation in developing rating scales, such as behaviorally anchored rating scales (BARS), automatically provides such training.

4 There are several methods that can be used for performance appraisal. These include trait approaches (such as graphic rating scales, mixed-standard scales, forced-choice forms, and essays), behavioral methods (such as critical incidents ratings, checklists, BARS, and BOS), and results methods (MBO). The choice of method depends on the purpose of the appraisal. Trait appraisals are simple to develop and complete, but they have problems of subjectivity and are not useful for feedback. Behavioral methods provide more specific information for giving feedback but can be time-consuming and costly to develop. Results appraisals are more objective and can link individual performance to the organization as a whole, but they may encourage a short-term perspective (e.g., annual goals) and may not include subtle yet important aspects of performance.

5 The degree to which the performance appraisal program benefits the organization and its members is directly related to the quality of the appraisal interviews that are conducted. Interviewing skills are best developed through instruction and supervised practice. Although there are various approaches to the interview, research suggests that employee participation and goal setting lead to higher satisfaction and improved performance. Discussing problems, showing support, minimizing criticism, and rewarding effective performance are also beneficial practices. In the interview, deficiencies in employee performance can be discussed and plans for improvement can be made.

REVIEW QUESTIONS

Multiple Choice

Choose the letter of the word or phrase that best completes each statement.

1 _____ 1. Research has shown that performance appraisals are used most widely as a basis for
   a. transfer.
   b. collective bargaining.
   c. assessment centers.
   d. compensation decisions.

1 _____ 2. One of the major benefits of a performance appraisal program is having a sound basis for
   a. peer appraisals.
   b. self-evaluation.
   c. improving performance.
   d. critical incident.

1 _____ 3. One of the objectives of supervisors in observing the day-to-day
                  performance of their employees is to develop a(n)
                  a. annual performance review.
                  b. job specification.
                  c. critical incident.
                  d. error of central tendency.

2 _____ 4. Before any performance appraisal is conducted, the standards by
                  which performance is to be evaluated should be clearly defined
                  and
                  a. communicated to the employee.
                  b. only then should training commence.
                  c. the error of central tendency communicated.
                  d. the halo error communicated.

2 _____ 5. The following basic considerations should be included in
                  establishing performance standards, **EXCEPT FOR**
                  a. strategic relevance.
                  b. criterion deficiency.
                  c. criterion contamination.
                  d. inconsistent performance.

2 _____ 6. When performance standards focus on a single criterion to the
                  exclusion of other important but less quantifiable performance
                  dimensions, the appraisal system is said to suffer from
                  a. leniency error.
                  b. strictness error.
                  c. criterion deficiency.
                  d. errors of central tendency.

2 _____ 7. The measure of stability or consistency of a standard, or the
                  extent to which individuals tend to maintain a certain level of
                  performance over time is
                  a. validity.
                  b. reliability.
                  c. critical incidence.
                  d. graphic rating.

2 _____ 8. The measure that permits managers to specify and communicate
                  precise information to employees regarding quality and quantity
                  output is called
                  a. reliability.
                  b. halo error.
                  c. graphic rating.
                  d. performance standards.

_____ 9. Having appraisals reviewed by a supervisor's superior reduces
   a. validity.
   b. biased evaluations.
   c. peer appraisals.
   d. performance.

_____ 10. Individuals of equal rank who work together are increasingly asked to evaluate each other is called
   a. team appraisal.
   b. 360-degree feedback.
   c. peer appraisal.
   d. customer appraisal.

_____ 11. A company's interest in team appraisals is frequently driven by its commitment to
   a. total quality management.
   b. management by objectives.
   c. strictness and leniency errors.
   d. central tendency.

_____ 12. The process that is intended to provide employees with as accurate a view of their performance as possible by getting input from others is called
   a. central tendency.
   b. critical incident.
   c. an assessment center.
   d. 360-degree feedback.

_____ 13. Raters who are reluctant to assign either extremely high or extremely low ratings commit the
   a. halo error.
   b. error of central tendency.
   c. strictness and leniency error.
   d. recency error.

_____ 14. When the appraisal is based largely on the employee's current behavior, good or bad, the rater has committed
   a. error of central tendency.
   b. recency error.
   c. contrast error.
   d. leniency or strictness error.

objective 3

_____ 15. When raters are required to rank employees from the best to the poorest, they are using a(n)
- a. error of central tendency.
- b. recency error.
- c. contrast error.
- d. leniency or strictness error.

objective 4

_____ 16. The performance appraisal method that focuses on the measurable contributions that employees make to the organization is a(n)
- a. behavioral approach.
- b. mixed standard scale.
- c. results-oriented approach.
- d. trait approach.

objective 4

_____ 17. A method of performance appraisal that is designed to measure the extent to which an employee possesses certain characteristics is called the
- a. forced-choice method.
- b. trait method.
- c. critical incident method.
- d. graphic rating-scale method.

objective 4

_____ 18. The performance appraisal method that requires the rater to choose from statements, often in pairs, that appear equally favorable or equally unfavorable is the
- a. forced-choice method.
- b. essay method.
- c. graphic rating-scale.
- d. mixed-standard scale.

objective 4

_____ 19. A performance appraisal where the appraiser is required to compose a statement that best describes the employee being appraised is the
- a. critical incident method.
- b. forced-choice method.
- c. mixed-standard scale.
- d. essay method.

objective 4

_____ 20. An unusual event that denotes superior or inferior employee performance in some part of the job is a(n)
- a. critical incident.
- b. management by objectives.
- c. halo error.
- d. essay method.

21. Rather than looking at the traits of employees or the behaviors they exhibit on the job, many organizations evaluate
    a. employee personalities.
    b. employee attributes.
    c. employee accomplishments.
    d. employee turnover.

22. A system involving a cycle that begins with setting the organization's common goals and objectives and ultimately returns to that step is called
    a. management by objectives.
    b. the critical incident method.
    c. the forced-choice method.
    d. the essay method.

23. The choice of method for a performance appraisal should be based largely on the
    a. critical incident.
    b. purpose of the appraisal.
    c. employee turnover.
    d. personality of the raters.

24. A format that attempts to give feedback to employees on their job performance and on planning for their future development is a(n)
    a. job description.
    b. critical incident.
    c. halo error.
    d. appraisal interview.

25. Norman R. F. Maier analyzes the cause-and-affect relationships in the following types of appraisal interviews **EXCEPT FOR**
    a. tell-and-sell.
    b. tell-and-listen.
    c. problem solving.
    d. self-assessment.

True/False

Identify the following statements as True or False.

1. From the standpoint of individual development, appraisal does not provide the feedback essential for strengths and weaknesses as well as improving performance.

objective 1   _____   2. If the support of top management is encouraged, the performance appraisal system still should be utilized without employee support.

objective 1   _____   3. An important principle of performance appraisal is continual feedback and employee coaching must be a positive daily activity.

objective 1   _____   4. By addressing employee concerns during the planning stage of the performance appraisal process, the organization will help the appraisal program to succeed in reaching its goals.

objective 1   _____   5. Organizational politics create fairness or equity in employee performance appraisals.

objective 1   _____   6. When performance standards are properly established, they do not help translate organizational goals and objectives into job requirements that convey acceptable and unacceptable levels of performance to employees.

objective 2   _____   7. Performance standards will permit managers to specify and communicate imprecise information to employees regarding quality and quantity of output.

objective 2   _____   8. Performance standards, when written, should be defined in quantifiable and measurable terms.

objective 2   _____   9. As the courts have made clear, a central issue in performance appraisal systems is to have carefully defined and measurable performance standards.

objective 2   _____   10. Employers might face legal challenges to their appraisal systems when appraisals indicate acceptable or above-average performance, but employees are passed over for promotion, disciplined for poor performance, or discharged.

objective 2   _____   11. To comply with the legal requirements of performance appraisals, employers must ensure that managers and supervisors document appraisals and reasons for subsequent human resource management actions.

objective 3   _____   12. Self-appraisal is detrimental when managers seek to increase an employee's involvement in the review process.

objective 3   _____   13. Self-appraisals may be best for administrative decisions rather than developmental purposes.

14. Subordinate appraisals give employees power over their bosses, making managers hesitant to endorse such a system, particularly when it might be used as a basis for compensation decisions.

15. One advantage of peer appraisals is the belief that they furnish less accurate and invalid information than appraisals by superiors.

16. Although 360-degree feedback can be useful for both developmental and administrative purposes, most companies start with an exclusive focus on development.

17. A weakness of many performance appraisal programs is that managers and supervisors are not adequately trained for the appraisal task and provide little meaningful feedback to subordinates.

18. Managers who give higher ratings because they believe an employee is "showing improvement" may unwittingly be committing recency error.

19. The fact that trait methods are the least popular method of performance appraisals is due in large part to the ease with which they are developed.

20. The mixed-standard scale of performance appraisal method is a modification of the basic behavior observation scale.

21. A major limitation of the essay method of performance appraisals is that composing an essay that attempts to cover all of an employee's essential characteristics is a very time-consuming task.

22. One of the potential advantages of a trait-oriented performance appraisal system is that traits tend to be subjective.

23. The appraisal interview gives a manager the opportunity to discuss a subordinate's performance record and to explore areas of possible improvement and growth.

24. Managers should assume that only one type of appraisal interview is appropriate for every review session.

25. The core purpose of a performance appraisal interview is to initiate a dialogue that will help an employee improve her or his performance.

Matching

Match each term with the proper definition.

Terms

a. behavior observation scale (BOS)
b. behaviorally anchored rating scale (BARS)
c. contrast error
d. critical incident
e. customer appraisal
f. error of central tendency
g. essay method
h. forced-choice method
i. graphic rating-scale method

j. leniency or strictness error
k. manager and/or supervisor appraisal
l. management by objectives (MBO)
m. mixed-standard scale method
n. peer appraisal
o. recency error
p. self-appraisal
q. similar-to-me error
r. subordinate appraisal
s. team appraisal

Definitions

_____ 1. performance-rating error in which the appraisal is based largely on the employee's most recent behavior, rather than on behavior throughout the appraisal period

_____ 2. philosophy of management that rates performance on the basis of employee achievement of goals set by the mutual agreement of employee and manager

_____ 3. performance appraisal, based on TQM concepts, that recognizes team accomplishment rather than individual performance

_____ 4. a behavioral approach to performance appraisal that measures the frequency of observed behavior

_____ 5. a trait approach to performance appraisal that requires the rater to compose a statement describing employee behavior

_____ 6. performance appraisal, which, like team appraisal, is based on TQM concepts and seeks evaluation from both external and internal customers

_____ 7. performance-rating error in which an employee's evaluation is biased either upward or downward because of comparison with another employee just previously evaluated

_____ 8. performance-rating error in which an appraiser inflates the evaluation of an employee because of a mutual personal connection

_____   9. a trait approach to performance appraisal whereby each employee is rated according to a scale of characteristics

_____   10. performance appraisal done by one's fellow employees that are generally compiled into a single profile to be used in the performance interview conducted by the employee's manager

_____   11. unusual event that denotes superior or inferior employee performance in some part of the job

_____   12. performance appraisal of a superior by an employee, that is more appropriate for developmental than for administrative purposes

_____   13. performance-rating error in which all employees are rated about average

_____   14. a trait approach to performance appraisal similar to other scale methods but based on comparison with (better than, equal to, or worse than) a standard

_____   15. a behavioral approach to performance appraisal that consists of a series of vertical scales, one for each important dimension of job performance

_____   16. performance appraisal done by the employee being evaluated, generally on an appraisal form completed by the employee prior to the performance interview

_____   17. performance appraisal done by an employee's manager and often reviewed by a manager one level higher

_____   18. a trait approach to performance appraisal that requires the rater to choose from statements designed to distinguish between successful and unsuccessful performance

_____   19. performance-rating error in which the appraiser tends to give employees either unusually high or unusually low ratings

Applications

 _____   1. Companies such as Best Buy and EDS have redesigned their performance appraisal systems to
                        a. include informal feedback and coaching sessions.
                        b. focus more on employee development and learning.
                        c. modify its MBO objectives.
                        d. increase employee assistance.

_____ 2. The concept that allows companies such as 3M and Buckman Laboratories to make objectives that 25 to 30 percent of their sales are to be generated from products developed within the past five years is known as
   a. strategic relevance.
   b. performance appraisal.
   c. job analysis.
   d. forced-choice method.

_____ 3. To evaluate employee performance, companies such as Cigna, Black & Decker, and Walt Disney Company use a 360-degree appraisal method also known as the
   a. halo error.
   b. multiple-rater approach.
   c. central tendency.
   d. leniency effect.

_____ 4. To reduce the subjective errors commonly made during the rating process, organizations such as Sears, Weyerhauser, and Allied Chemical have developed
   a. performance analysis.
   b. labor contracts.
   c. training programs.
   d. job evaluation.

_____ 5. Companies such as AT&T, Weyerhauser, and Dayton-Hudson have used the BOS (Behavior Observation Scales) and research shows that users of this system prefer it over the
   a. essay method.
   b. ranking method.
   c. MBO system.
   d. BARS or trait scale.

How to Prepare for a Performance Appraisal Interview

A student should understand the objective of performance appraisal. Employees need feedback to understand how secure one is within the organization. It is important the employee has knowledge of the work activity required in performing their job. A performance appraisal interview will accomplish such objectives.

A performance appraisal is conducted to assess the performance of the individual in his/her job operations. There are different performance appraisal methods and different means to establish this activity. The traditional means is a supervisor evaluating the performance of the employee. There are also peer, self, and customer methods of undertaking performance appraisals.

In the traditional method of interviewing, the supervisor should have a thorough understanding of the employee's job description. In addition, the performance appraisal should be reduced to writing and taken into the interview with the supervisor. The appraisal should be used as a basis for merit reviews and should be signed at the end of the interview. This is to indicate the supervisor has gone over the performance appraisal. Finally, there should be an appeal process if the employee disagrees with the appraisal.

SOLUTIONS

Multiple Choice:	True/False:	Matching:
1. d	1. False	1. o
2. c	2. False	2. l
3. a	3. True	3. s
4. a	4. True	4. a
5. d	5. False	5. g
6. c	6. False	6. e
7. b	7. False	7. c
8. d	8. True	8. q
9. b	9. True	9. i
10. c	10. True	10. n
11. a	11. True	11. d
12. d	12. False	12. r
13. b	13. False	13. f
14. b	14. True	14. m
15. c	15. False	15. b
16. c	16. True	16. p
17. b	17. True	17. k
18. a	18. True	18. h
19. d	19. False	19. j
20. a	20. False	
21. c	21. True	
22. a	22. False	
23. b	23. True	
24. d	24. False	
25. d	25. True	

False Statements from True/False

1. From the standpoint of individual development, appraisal **provides** the feedback essential for strengths and weaknesses as well as improving performance.
2. If the support of top management is encouraged, the performance appraisal system **will not be successful**.
5. Organizational politics **can introduce a bias even in fairly administered** in employee performance appraisals.
6. When performance standards are properly established, they **help** translate organizational goals and objectives into job requirements that convey acceptable and unacceptable levels of performance to employees.
7. Performance standards will permit managers to specify and communicate **precise** information to employees regarding quality and quantity of output.
12. Self-appraisal is **beneficial** when managers seek to increase an employee's involvement in the review process.

13. Self-appraisals may be best for **developmental purposes** rather than **administrative decisions**.

15. One advantage of peer appraisals is the belief that they furnish **more** accurate and **valid** information than appraisals by superiors.

19. The fact that trait methods are the **most** popular method of performance appraisals is due in large part to the ease with which they are developed.

20. The mixed-standard scale of performance appraisal method is a modification of the basic **rating-scale method**.

22. One of the potential **drawbacks** of a trait-oriented performance appraisal system is that traits tend to be subjective.

24. Managers should **not** assume that only one type of appraisal interview is appropriate for every review session.

Applications

1. b
2. a
3. b
4. c
5. d

CHAPTER 9

MANAGING COMPENSATION

Employees seek various psychological rewards from their jobs, but this does not diminish the importance of the compensation they receive. It is essential that this compensation be equitable in terms of the job's value to the organization and in relation to the pay other employees receive. The purchasing power of workers' salaries must be adjusted upward periodically to accommodate rises in the cost of living. In addition, compensation payments must be consistent with the terms of the labor agreement, where one exists, and with state and federal regulations governing it. Issues of equal pay for comparable worth, pay compression, and low wage budgets are emerging issues in the field of management compensation.

LEARNING OBJECTIVES

After studying this chapter you should be able to

 Explain employer concerns in developing a strategic compensation program.

 Indicate the various factors that influence the setting of wages.

 Differentiate the mechanics of each of the major job evaluation systems.

 Explain the purpose of a wage survey.

 Define the wage curve, pay grades, and rate ranges as parts of the compensation structure.

 Identify the major provisions of the federal laws affecting compensation.

Discuss the current issues of equal pay for comparable worth, pay compression and low wage budgets.

CHAPTER SUMMARY RELATING TO LEARNING OBJECTIVES

Establishing compensation programs requires both large and small organizations to consider specific goals—employee retention, compensation distribution, and adherence to a budget, for instance. Compensation must reward employees for past efforts (pay-for-performance) while serving to motivate employees' future performance. Internal and external equity of the pay program affects employees' concepts of fairness. Organizations must balance each of these concerns while still remaining competitive. The ability to attract qualified employees while controlling labor costs is a major factor in allowing organizations to remain viable in the domestic or international markets.

The basis on which compensation payments are determined, and the way they are administered, can significantly affect employee productivity and the achievement of organizational goals. Internal influences include the employer's compensation policy, the worth of the job, the performance of the employee, and the employer's ability to pay. External factors influencing wage rates include labor market conditions, area wage rates, cost of living, the outcomes of collective bargaining, and legal requirements.

Organizations use one of four basic job evaluation techniques to determine the relative worth of jobs. The job ranking system arranges jobs in numerical order on the basis of the importance of the job's duties and responsibilities to the organization. The job classification system slots jobs into pre-established grades. Higher-rated grades will require more responsibilities, working conditions, and job duties. The point system of job evaluation uses a point scheme based upon the compensable job factors of skill, effort, responsibility, and working conditions. The more compensable factors a job possesses, the more points are assigned to it. Jobs with higher accumulated points are considered more valuable to the organization. The factor comparison system evaluates jobs on a factor-by-factor basis against key jobs in the organization.

Wage surveys determine the external equity of jobs. Data obtained from surveys will facilitate establishing the organization's wage policy while ensuring that the employer does not pay more, or less, than needed for jobs in the relevant labor market.

The wage structure is composed of the wage curve, pay grades, and rate ranges. The wage curve depicts graphically the pay rates assigned to jobs within each pay grade. Pay grades represent the grouping of similar jobs on the basis of their relative worth. Each pay grade will include a rate range. Rate ranges will have a midpoint and minimum and maximum pay rates for all jobs in the pay grade.

6 Both the Davis-Bacon Act and the Walsh-Healy Act are prevailing wage statutes. These laws require government contractors to pay wages normally based on the union scale in the employer's operating area. The Walsh-Healy Act also requires payment of 12 the regular pay for hours over eight per day or forty per week. The Fair Labor Standards Act contains provisions covering the federal minimum wage, hours worked, and child labor.

7 The concept of comparable worth seeks to overcome the fact that jobs held by women are compensated at a lower rate than those performed by men. This happens even though both types of jobs may contribute equally to organizational productivity. Wage-rate compression largely affects managerial and senior employees as the pay given to new employees or the wage increases gained through union agreements erode the pay differences between these groups. Living wage laws seek to pay employees at a level that will allow them to maintain an acceptable standard of living. Low wage increases are a prominent compensation strategy as employers seek to adjust to competitive challenges.

REVIEW QUESTIONS

Multiple Choice

Choose the letter of the word or phrase that best completes each statement.

1 _____ 1. Linking compensation to organizational objectives, the pay-for-performance standard, and the motivating value of compensation are aspects of
a. job enlargement.
b. strategic compensation planning.
c. job enrichment.
d. employee empowerment.

1 _____ 2. A program in which components of the compensation package create value for the organization and its employees is
a. value-added compensation.
b. pay-for-performance standard.
c. pay equity.
d. competence-based pay.

1 _____ 3. A wide range of compensation options, including merit-based pay, bonuses, salary commissions, job and pay banding, team/group incentives, and various gainsharing programs, is called
a. job evaluation.
b. performance appraisal.
c. pay-for-performance.
d. management by objectives.

4. When employees believe that the wage rates for their jobs approximate the job's worth to the organization, compensation policies are considered to be
   a. mixed combinations.
   b. externally equitable.
   c. paired comparisons.
   d. internally equitable.

5. The concept that exists when an organization is paying wages that are relatively equal to what other employers are paying for similar types of work is known as
   a. external pay equity.
   b. comparable worth.
   c. internal pay equity.
   d. equity theory of motivation.

6. The theory that predicts how one's level of motivation depends on the attractiveness of the rewards sought and the probability of obtaining those rewards is the
   a. two-factor theory of motivation.
   b. equity theory of motivation.
   c. expectancy theory of motivation.
   d. needs hierarchy theory.

7. A system of pay in which employees are paid according to the number of units they produce is
   a. hourly work.
   b. salary.
   c. piecework.
   d. real wages.

8. In both hourly and salary jobs, differences in employee performance can be recognized and rewarded through promotion and with various
   a. child care programs.
   b. job evaluation programs.
   c. job analysis programs.
   d. incentive programs.

9. A means of wage payment that can be affected by earned profits and other financial resources available to employers is a(n)
   a. employee worth.
   b. pay level.
   c. critical incident.
   d. job evaluation program.

2

_____ 10. Due to inflation, compensation rates have been adjusted upward periodically to help employees maintain their
- a. comparable worth.
- b. job evaluation.
- c. purchasing power.
- d. non-economic benefits.

3

_____ 11. Wage increases larger than rises in the consumer price index are
- a. real wages.
- b. red circle rates.
- c. pay equity.
- d. comparable worth.

3

_____ 12. One important component of the wage mix to an employer is the
- a. worth of the job.
- b. escalator clause.
- c. inflationary spiral.
- d. equity theory of motivation.

3

_____ 13. The job evaluation method in which compensable factors of the job to be evaluated are compared against the compensable factors of key jobs within the organization is known as the
- a. Hay profile method.
- b. job ranking system.
- c. job classification system.
- d. factor comparison system.

3

_____ 14. A job evaluation system that has been developed specifically to evaluate executive, managerial, and professional positions is the
- a. essay method.
- b. forced-choice method.
- c. critical incidents method.
- d. Hay profile method.

3

_____ 15. Job evaluation systems provide for internal equity and serve as the basis for
- a. wage-rate determination.
- b. performance appraisal.
- c. job analysis.
- d. comparable worth issues.

4

_____ 16. A major national publisher of wage and salary data is the
- a. Chamber of Commerce.
- b. Bureau of Labor Statistics.
- c. Internal Revenue Service.
- d. Local Employer Association.

17. The relationship between the relative worth of employees' jobs and their wage rates can be represented by means of a(n)
    a. escalator clause.
    b. comparable worth.
    c. wage curve.
    d. job ranking system.

18. Wages paid above the range maximum are called
    a. competence-based pay.
    b. comparable worth.
    c. red circle rates.
    d. wage-rate compression.

19. The method that compensates employees for the different skills or increased knowledge they possess rather than for the job they hold in a designated job category is known as
    a. broadbanding.
    b. competence-based pay.
    c. job enlargement.
    d. pay-for-performance.

20. The concept in which organizations adopt a competence-based pay system to structure their compensation payments to employees is
    a. broadbanding.
    b. external pay equity.
    c. job enrichment.
    d. job enlargement.

21. The major provisions of the Fair Labor Standards Act include the following, **EXCEPT FOR**
    a. equal pay for equal work.
    b. minimum wage rates.
    c. overtime payments.
    d. child labor.

22. The concept in which jobs historically held exclusively by men and by women are considered equal in terms of value or worth to the employer is known as
    a. sexual harassment.
    b. job evaluation.
    c. comparable worth.
    d. external pay equity.

23. The internal pay-equity concern that results in the reduction of differences between job classes is
    a. employee empowerment.
    b. job enlargement.
    c. job specification.
    d. wage-rate compression.

24. Laws that require contractors who work for local governments or private employers that receive government subsidies or tax breaks must pay employees an income above the federal poverty level are called _____ laws.
    a. low wage.
    b. living-wage.
    c. real wage.
    d. high wage.

25. Unfavorable effects for employers and society such as increased employee turnover and diminished employee output may be a result of
    a. low wages.
    b. high wages.
    c. real wages.
    d. wage-rate compression.

True/False

Identify the following statements as True or False.

1. Pay equity is achieved when the compensation received is unequal to the value of the work performed.

2. Work performed in most private, public, and not-for-profit organizations has traditionally been compensated on a professionally contracted basis.

3. Salaried employees are generally paid the same for each pay period, even though they occasionally may work more hours or fewer than the regular number of hours in a period.

4. Managers and supervisors as well as a large number of white-collar employees are in the non-exempt category of pay structure.

5. Economic conditions and competition faced by employers do not significantly affect the rates they are able to pay.

objective 2   _____   6. The major external factors that influence wage rates include labor market conditions, area wage rates, cost of living, legal requirements, and the employer's ability to pay.

objective 2   _____   7. The Consumer Price Index (CPI) is based on prices of food, clothing, shelter, and fuels; transportation fares; charges for medical services; and prices of other goods and services that people buy for day-to-day living.

objective 3   _____   8. All job evaluation methods require the same consistent degree of managerial judgement.

objective 3   _____   9. Job ranking can be done by a single individual who has a working knowledge of all jobs; however, it should never be done by a committee composed of management and employee representatives.

objective 3   _____   10. The basic weakness of the job ranking system is that it does not provide a very refined measure of each job's worth.

objective 3   _____   11. The principle advantage of the point system job evaluation technique is that it provides a more refined basis for making judgments than either the ranking or classification systems.

objective 3   _____   12. The factor comparison system differs from the point system in that a job's compensable factors are compared against the compensable factors of key jobs within the organization.

objective 4   _____   13. Many states conduct wage and salary surveys on either a municipal or county basis and make them available to the Internal Revenue Service.

objective 5   _____   14. A wage curve may be constructed graphically by preparing a scatter-gram, which consists of a series of dots that represent the current inflation rates.

objective 5   _____   15. From an administrative standpoint, it is generally preferable to group jobs into pay grades and to pay all jobs within a particular grade a different rate or rate range.

objective 5   _____   16. Very few salary structures provide for the ranges of adjoining pay grades to overlap.

objective 5   _____   17. The final step in setting up a wage structure is to determine the appropriate pay grade into which each job should be placed on the basis of its evaluated worth.

6 _____ 18. Broadbanding uses many traditional salary grades for employee compensation.

6 _____ 19. The three principle federal laws affecting wages are the Davis-Bacon Act, the Walsh-Healy Act, and the Fair Labor Standards Act.

6 _____ 20. Under the Fair Labor Standards Act, employers are not required to pay time-and-a-half wages for hours worked in excess of forty hours in any particular week.

6 _____ 21. The four employee groups that are excluded from overtime provisions are secretaries, administrators, professionals, and outside salespersons.

7 _____ 22. As managers strive to reward employees in a fair manner, they must consider controls over labor costs, legal issues regarding male and female wage payments, and external pay-equity concerns.

7 _____ 23. There are several causes for wage-rate compression, which include job analysis, job evaluation, and performance appraisal.

7 _____ 24. Wage-rate compression often occurs when organizations grant pay adjustments for lower-rated jobs without providing commensurate adjustments for occupations at the top of the job hierarchy.

7 _____ 25. The strongest opposition against living-wage laws comes from high wage employers.

Matching

Match each term with the proper definition.

Terms

a. comparable worth
b. consumer price index (CPI)
c. escalator clauses
d. exempt employees
e. factor comparison system
f. Hay profile method
g. hourly work
h. job classification system
i. job evaluation
j. job ranking system
k. nonexempt employees
l. pay equity

m. pay-for-performance standard
n. pay grades
o. piecework
p. point system
q. real wages
r. red circle rates
s. competence-based pay
t. value-added compensation
u. wage and salary survey
v. wage curve
w. wage-rate compression

Definitions

_____ 1. curve in a scatter-gram representing the relationship between the relative worth of jobs and their wage rates

_____ 2. quantitative job evaluation procedure that determines the relative value of a job by the total points assigned to it

_____ 3. standard by which managers tie compensation to employee effort and performance

_____ 4. job evaluation system that permits the evaluation process to be accomplished on a factor-by-factor basis

_____ 5. the concept in which dissimilar jobs often held exclusively by males and females, equal in terms of value or worth to the employer, should be paid the same

_____ 6. clauses in labor agreements that provide for quarterly cost-of-living adjustment in wages, basing the adjustments on changes in the consumer price index

_____ 7. an employee's perception that compensation received is equal to the value of the work performed

_____ 8. compression of differentials between job classes, particularly the differential between hourly workers and their managers

_____ 9. work paid on an hourly basis

_____ 10. groups of jobs within a particular class that are paid the same rate or rate range

_____ 11. work paid according to the number of units produced

_____ 12. employees not covered by the overtime provisions of the Fair Labor Standards Act

_____ 13. measure of the average change in prices over time in a fixed "market basket" of goods and services

_____ 14. systematic process of determining the relative worth of jobs in order to establish which jobs should be paid more than others within an organization

_____ 15. job evaluation technique using three factors, knowledge, mental activity, and accountability, to evaluate executive and managerial positions

_____ 16. questionnaire of the wages paid to employees of other employers in the organization's relevant labor market

_____ 17. wage increases larger than rises in the consumer price index

_____ 18. simplest and oldest system of job evaluation by which jobs are arrayed on the basis of their relative worth

_____ 19. compensates employees for the different skills or increased knowledge they possess rather than for the job they hold

_____ 20. employees covered by the overtime provisions of the Fair Labor Standards Act

_____ 21. system of job evaluation by which jobs are classified and grouped according to a series of predetermined wage grades

_____ 22. evaluating the individual components of the compensation program to see if they advance the needs of employees and the goals of the organization

_____ 23. payment rates above the maximum of the pay range

Applications

1. The pay objective of Preventive Health Care is to be an industry pay leader and is reflected in its
   a. job evaluation program.
   b. compensation policy.
   c. external equity program.
   d. factor comparison system.

2. Companies, such as Levi Strauss and Dell Computer, use job evaluation in establishing
   a. performance appraisals.
   b. job analysis.
   c. critical incidents.
   d. wage structures.

3. A quantitative job evaluation procedure used at Digital Equipment, TRW, Johnson Wax Company, and many other public and private organizations to determine the relative value of a job is the
   a. point system.
   b. ranking method.
   c. Hay profile method.
   d. job classification system.

4. A job payment plan instituted at Nortel Network, Sherwin-Williams, and Honeywell, which compensates employees based on their knowledge rather than for the job they hold in a designated category, is known as
   a. external pay equity.
   b. expectancy theory of motivation.
   c. comparable worth.
   d. competence-based pay.

5. The law that attempts to create wage parity for women in the labor force is the
   a. Fair Labor Standards Act.
   b. Age Discrimination in Employment Act.
   c. Equal Pay Act.
   d. Civil Rights Act.

How to Negotiate a Fair Compensation Package

Research the job market for compensation or salary ranges for a graduating student in the field of business.

Wages and fringe benefits are important to present to a prospective employer. To gain access to this type of information visit the college placement office, local chamber of commerce, library, or the Internet.

In negotiating a fair compensation package with an employer, the student should have an understanding of his/her economic needs. A salary range is recommended when a potential employer asks the starting salary requirements. Know his/her salary objectives and career goals when interviewing with an employer. Following the interview, have questions ready concerning salary objectives and career development opportunities. Utilize previous job experience as a bargaining tool for obtaining a higher starting salary. Apply your marketing knowledge to project a positive image in the interview.

SOLUTIONS

Multiple Choice:	True/False:	Matching:
1. b	1. False	1. v
2. a	2. False	2. p
3. c	3. True	3. m
4. d	4. False	4. e
5. a	5. False	5. a
6. c	6. False	6. c
7. c	7. True	7. l
8. d	8. False	8. w
9. b	9. False	9. g
10. c	10. True	10. n
11. a	11. True	11. o
12. a	12. True	12. d
13. d	13. False	13. b
14. d	14. False	14. i
15. a	15. False	15. f
16. b	16. False	16. u
17. c	17. True	17. q
18. c	18. False	18. j
19. b	19. True	19. s
20. a	20. False	20. k
21. a	21. False	21. h
22. c	22. False	22. t
23. d	23. False	23. r
24. b	24. True	
25. a	25. False	

False Statements from True/False

1. Pay equity is achieved when the compensation received is **equal** to the value of the work performed.
2. Work performed in most private, public, and not-for-profit organizations has traditionally been compensated on **an hourly** basis.
4. Managers and supervisors as well as a large number of white-collar employees are in the **exempt** category of pay structure.
5. Economic conditions and competition faced by employers **significantly** affect the rates they are able to pay.
6. The major external factors that influence wage rates include labor market conditions, area wage rates, cost of living, legal requirements, and **collective bargaining if the employer is unionized.**
8. All job evaluation methods require **varying degrees** of managerial judgment.
9. Job ranking can be done by a single individual who has a working knowledge of all jobs, **or by** a committee composed of management and employee representatives.

13. Many states conduct wage and salary surveys on **local, regional, or national** organizations and make them available to the Internal Revenue Service.
14. A wage curve may be constructed graphically by preparing a scatter-gram, which consists of a series of dots that represent the current **wage** rates.
15. From an administrative standpoint, it is generally preferable to group jobs into pay grades and to pay all jobs within a particular grade **the same** rate or rate range.
16. **Most** salary structures provide for the ranges of adjoining pay grades to overlap.
18. Broadbanding **collapses** many traditional salary grades **into a few wide salary bands**.
20. Under the Fair Labor Standards Act, employers **are** required to pay time-and-a-half wages for hours worked in excess of forty hours in any particular week.
21. The four employee groups that are excluded from overtime provisions are **executives**, administrators, professionals, and outside salespersons.
22. As managers strive to reward employees in a fair manner, they must consider controls over labor costs, legal issues regarding male and female wage payments, and **internal** pay-equity concerns.
23. There are several causes for wage-rate compression, which include **when unions negotiate across-the-board increases for hourly employees but managerial personnel are not granted corresponding wage differentials, or scarcity of applicants.**
25. The strongest opposition against living-wage laws comes from **low** wage employers.

Applications

1. b
2. d
3. a
4. d
5. c

CHAPTER 10

INCENTIVE REWARDS

Compensation can be a significant source of motivation if at least part of it is tied directly to the employee's performance. Countless financial incentive systems have been developed over the years to motivate employees who occupy various levels within an organization and who perform different types of duties. Some of these systems have been successful, while others have not. The success of a particular system depends not so much on the formula for determining incentive payments, as on the existence of a favorable climate in which the system can operate. Success also depends on the degree to which the system has been tailored to the needs of the organization where it is to be used. Contributing to this success, furthermore, are the ways in which the system allows for employees to participate, psychologically as well as financially, in the organization. A rather new form of compensation, employee stock ownership plans, can be advantageous to employers and to employees.

LEARNING OBJECTIVES

After studying this chapter you should be able to

 Discuss the basic requirements for successful implementation of incentive programs.

 Identify the types of, and reasons for implementing, individual incentive plans.

 Explain why merit raises may fail to motivate employees adequately and discuss ways to increase their motivational value.

 Indicate the advantage of each of the principal methods used to compensate salespersons.

 Differentiate how gains may be shared with employees under the Scanlon, Rucker, and Improshare, and earnings-at-risk gainsharing systems.

Differentiate between profit-sharing plans and explain advantages and disadvantages of these programs.

Describe the main types of employee stock ownership plans and discuss the advantages of employee stock ownership plans to employers and employees.

CHAPTER SUMMARY RELATING TO LEARNING OBJECTIVES

1 The success of an incentive pay plan depends on the organizational climate in which it must operate, employee confidence in it, and its suitability to employee and organizational needs. Importantly, employees must view their incentive pay as being equitable and related to their performance. Performance measures should be quantifiable, easily understood, and bear a demonstrated relationship to organizational performance.

2 Piecework plans pay employees a given rate for each unit satisfactorily completed. Employers implement these plans when output is easily measured and when the production process is fairly standardized. Bonuses are incentive payments above base wages paid on either an individual or team basis. A bonus is offered to encourage employees to exert greater effort. Standard hour plans establish a standard time for job completion. An incentive is paid for finishing the job in less than the preestablished time. The plans are popular for jobs with a fixed time for completion.

3 Merit raises will not serve to motivate employees when they are seen as entitlements, which occur when these raises are given yearly without regard to changes in employee performance. Merit raises are not motivational when they are given because of seniority or favoritism or when merit budgets are inadequate to sufficiently reward employee performance. To be motivational, merit raises must be such that employees see a clear relationship between pay and performance and the salary increase must be large enough to exceed inflation and higher income taxes.

4 Sales persons may be compensated by a straight salary, a combination of salary and commission, or a commission only. Paying employees a straight salary allows them to focus on tasks other than sales, such as service and customer goodwill. A straight commission plan causes employees to emphasize sales goals. A combination of salary and commission provides the advantages of both straight salary and the straight commission form of payments.

5 The Scanlon, Rucker, Improshare, and earnings-at-risk gainshare plans pay bonuses to employees unrelated to profit levels. Each of these plans encourages employees to maximize their performance and cooperation through suggestions offered to improve organizational performance. The Scanlon Plan pays an employee a bonus based on saved labor cost measured against the organization's sales value of production. The bonus under the Rucker Plan is based on any improvement in the relationship between the total earnings of hourly employees and the value of production that employees create. The Improshare bonus is paid when employees increase production output above a given target level. With the earnings-at-risk program, employees earn bonuses when production quotas are met or exceeded, as well as wages that have been put at risk.

6 Profit-sharing plans pay to employees sums of money based on the organization's profits. Cash payments are made to eligible employees at specified times, normally yearly. The primary purpose of profit sharing is to provide employees with additional income through their participation in organizational achievement. Employee commitment to improved productivity, quality, and customer service will contribute to organizational success and, in turn, to their compensation. Profit-sharing plans may not achieve their stated gains when employee performance is unrelated to organizational success or failure. This may occur because of economic conditions, other competition, or environmental conditions. Profit-sharing plans can have a negative effect on employee morale when plans fail to consistently reward employees.

7 With a stock bonus employee stock ownership plan, each year the organization contributes stock or cash to buy stock that is placed in an employee stock ownership plan trust. With a leveraged employee stock ownership plan, the organization borrows money from a lending institution to purchase stock for the trust. With either plan, the employee stock ownership plan holds the stock for employees until they either retire or leave the company, at which time the stock is sold back to the company or through a brokerage firm. Employers receive tax benefits for qualified employee stock ownership plans; they also hope to receive their employees' commitment to organizational improvement. Employees, however, may lose their retirement income should the company fail or stock prices fall. Another drawback to employee stock ownership plans is that they are not guaranteed by any federal agency.

REVIEW QUESTIONS

Multiple Choice

Choose the letter of the word or phrase that best completes each statement.

_____ 1. A clear trend in strategic compensation management is the growth of
   a. traditional pay plans.
   b. incentive plans.
   c. obsolescent piece-rate systems.
   d. antiquated group incentive systems.

_____ 2. Managers believe that employees will assume ownership of their jobs, thereby improving their effort and overall job performance, by meshing
   a. traditional pay plans to those of employer associations.
   b. compensation with that of the competition.
   c. compensation and organizational objectives.
   d. compensation programs to those outside the industry.

_____ 3. The success of an incentive plan depends on the firm's
   a. internal organizational environment.
   b. external organizational resources.
   c. philosophy of organized labor.
   d. organizational structure.

_____ 4. Management should never allow incentive payments to be seen as a(n)
   a. bonus.
   b. variable pay.
   c. entitlement.
   d. reward.

_____ 5. The following impact the organization's choice of incentive pay plans, **EXCEPT FOR**
   a. technology.
   b. job tasks and duties.
   c. organizational goals.
   d. social orientation.

6. Employees whose production exceeds the standard output receive a higher rate for all of their work than the rate paid to those who do not exceed the standard under a
    a. holidays and vacations.
    b. differential piece rate.
    c. career curve.
    d. socialization process.

7. A plan that sets incentive rates on the basis of a predetermined standard time for completing a job is known as the
    a. combined salary and commission plan.
    b. piece rate incentive plan.
    c. standard hour plan.
    d. street commission plan.

8. An annual payment that is supplemental to the basic wage for employees is a
    a. contracted wage.
    b. fringe benefit.
    c. differential piece rate.
    d. bonus.

9. A raise that links an increase in base pay to how successfully an employee performs his or her job is a
    a. merit pay program.
    b. combined salary and commission plan.
    c. Rucker Plan.
    d. Scanlon Plan.

10. One of the major weakness of merit raises lies in increases based on a
    a. performance appraisal system.
    b. differential piece rate.
    c. straight commission plan.
    d. competitive benchmarking.

11. A method of pay where employers receive a year-end merit payment which is not added to their base pay is called a
    a. combined salary and commission plan.
    b. lump-sum merit program.
    c. team incentive plan.
    d. gainsharing plan.

12. A sales incentive plan that is based on a percentage of sales and provides maximum incentive for the salesperson is the
    a. straight salary plan.
    b. combined salary and commission plan.
    c. Scanlon Plan.
    d. straight commission plan.

13. The following are disadvantages of the straight commission plan, **EXCEPT FOR**
    a. increased emphasis on sales volume than profits.
    b. increased incentive to sell.
    c. disregard for customer service.
    d. higher turnover of trained salespersons in poor sales periods.

14. The following are the bases for computing executive salaries, **EXCEPT FOR**
    a. compensation to union officials.
    b. organization size.
    c. sales volume.
    d. industry grouping.

15. A bonus payment to an executive usually takes the form of
    a. increased health benefits and vacation time.
    b. increased personal days and sick days.
    c. increased holidays and compensatory time.
    d. cash or stock.

16. A major long-term incentive for an executive is a(n)
    a. piece-rate incentive.
    b. stock price appreciation grant.
    c. annual bonus.
    d. combined salary and commission plan.

17. One means of demonstrating the executive's importance to the organization while giving him/her an incentive to improve performance is a
    a. differential piece rate.
    b. career curve.
    c. perk.
    d. straight salary initiative.

18. The two bonus plans, the Scanlon Plan and the Rucker Plan, both emphasize
    a. participative management.
    b. economic forecasts.
    c. supplemental pay benefits.
    d. competitive reactions.

19. The type of bonus plan in which employees offer ideas and suggestions to improve productivity in the plant and are then rewarded for their constructive efforts is the
    a. annual bonus plan.
    b. Scanlon Plan.
    c. day-rate plan.
    d. combined salary and commission plan.

20. The bonus incentive plan based on the historic relationship between total earnings of hourly employees and the production value created by the employees is known as the
    a. Scanlon Plan.
    b. combined salary and commission plan.
    c. straight salary plan.
    d. Rucker Plan.

21. A gainsharing program based upon overall productivity of the work team is called a(n)
    a. competition benchmarking.
    b. team incentive plan.
    c. earnings-at-risk incentive plan.
    d. improshare.

22. An incentive plan that allows employees to recapture lower wages or reap additional income above full base pay when quality, service, or productivity goals are met or exceeded is the
    a. Improshare plan.
    b. earnings-at-risk plan.
    c. Scanlon Plan.
    d. Rucker Plan.

23. Any procedure in which an employer pays all regular employees special current or deferred sums based upon the profits of the enterprise is
    a. profit-sharing plan.
    b. gainsharing.
    c. Scanlon plan.
    d. piecerate plan.

6   _____ 24. An incentive plan that gives employees the opportunity to
                        increase their earnings by contributing to the growth of their
                        organization's profits is known as a
                        a. straight commission plan.
                        b. straight salary plan.
                        c. combined salary and commission plan.
                        d. profit-sharing plan.

7   _____ 25. The type of incentive that may take the form of a stock bonus plan
                        or a leveraged plan is the
                        a. employee stock ownership plan.
                        b. Rucker Plan.
                        c. Scanlon Plan.
                        d. combined salary and commission plan.

True/False

Identify the following statements as True or False.

1   _____   1. Incentive plans always satisfy employee needs as well as the
                        organization's needs.

1   _____   2. The primary purpose of an incentive compensation plan is to pay-
                        off under all circumstances, however the level of motivation is not
                        relevant.

2   _____   3. One of the newest incentive plans is based on piecework.

2   _____   4. Straight piecework employees receive a varying rate of pay for
                        each unit produced.

2   _____   5. One of the most significant weaknesses of piecework, as well as
                        other incentive plans based on individual effort, is that it may not
                        always be an effective motivator.

2   _____   6. Piecework is appropriate where quality is more important than
                        quantity.

2   _____   7. Bonuses may be determined on the basis of cost reduction,
                        quality improvement, or performance criteria established by the
                        organization.

3   _____   8. Employees in some organizations are opposed to merit raises
                        because they do not really trust management.

objective 3   _____   9. For employees, the lump-sum merit program provides financial control by maintaining annual salary expenses at fixed rates of production.

objective 4   _____   10. The percentage of cash compensation paid out in commissions is called leverage.

objective 4   _____   11. Professional employees can receive compensation beyond base pay in the form of piecework.

objective 4   _____   12. Organizations commonly have more than one compensation strategy for executives in order to meet various organizational goals and executive needs.

objective 4   _____   13. Most organizations pay their short-term incentive bonuses in the form of common stock to maintain their pay-for-performance strategy.

objective 4   _____   14. Balanced scorecards in terms of executive incentives are used to measure customer satisfaction, employee salary, and product or service leadership.

objective 4   _____   15. Gainsharing plans enable employees to share in the benefits of improved efficiency realized by the organization or major units within it.

objective 5   _____   16. Both the Scanlon Plan and the Rucker Plan emphasize participative management.

objective 5   _____   17. Under the Scanlon Plan, financial incentives based on increases in employee productivity are not offered to all employees, only executives.

objective 5   _____   18. The Rucker Plan may only be used to cover production workers.

objective 5   _____   19. The financial incentive of the Rucker Plan is based on the historic relationship between the total earnings of employers and the production value that employers create.

objective 5   _____   20. Improshare output is measured by the number of finished products that a work team produces in a given period.

objective 5   _____   21. Improshare is a bonus plan based on dollar savings much like the Scanlon and Rucker Plans.

objective 5   _____   22. Earnings-at-risk incentive plans place a portion of an employee's base pay at risk.

6 _____ 23. The purpose of profit sharing is to have employees commit to a specific area of the organization.

6 _____ 24. Employee stock ownership programs are more likely to serve their intended purposes in privately held companies than in publicly held ones.

6 _____ 25. Although studies show that productivity improves when employee stock ownership plans are implemented, these gains are not guaranteed.

Matching

Match each term with the proper definition.

Terms

a. bonus
b. combined salary and commission plan
c. differential piece rate
d. earnings-at-risk incentive plans
e. employee stock ownership plans (ESOPs)
f. gainsharing plans
g. Improshare
h. lump-sum merit program
i. merit guidelines
j. perquisites

k. profit sharing
l. Rucker Plan
m. Scanlon Plan
n. spot bonus
o. standard hour plan
p. straight commission plan
q. straight piecework
r. straight salary plan
s. team incentive plan
t. variable pay

Definitions

_____ 1. gainsharing program under which bonuses are based on the overall productivity of the work team

_____ 2. compensation plan based on a percentage of sales

_____ 3. guidelines for awarding merit raises that are tied to performance objectives

_____ 4. incentive payment that is supplemental to the base wage

_____ 5. compensation plan that permits salespeople to be paid for performing various duties that are not reflected immediately in their sales volume

_____   6. bonus incentive plan based on the historic relationship between the total
                earnings of hourly employees and the production value created by the
                employees

_____   7. stock plans in which an organization contributes shares of its stock to an
                established trust for the purpose of stock purchases by its employees

_____   8. unplanned bonus given for employee effort unrelated to an established
                performance measure

_____   9. compensation plan that includes a straight salary and a commission

_____ 10. special benefits often given to executives

_____ 11. programs under which both employees and the organization share the
                financial gains according to a predetermined formula that reflects
                improved productivity and profitability

_____ 12. compensation rate under which employees whose production exceeds
                the standard amount of output receive a higher rate for all of their work
                than the rate paid to those who do not exceed the standard amount

_____ 13. compensation plan where all team members receive an incentive bonus
                payment when production or service standards are met or exceeded

_____ 14. incentive plan that sets rates based on the completion of a job in a
                predetermined standard time

_____ 15. program under which employees receive a year-end merit payment that is
                not added to their base pay

_____ 16. incentive pay plans placing a portion of the employee's base pay at risk,
                but giving the opportunity to earn income above base pay when goals are
                met or exceeded

_____ 17. bonus incentive plan using employee and management committees to
                gain cost-reduction improvements

_____ 18. any procedure by which an employer pays or makes available to all
                regular employees, in addition to base pay, special current or deferred
                sums based on the profits of the enterprise

_____ 19. incentive plan under which employees receive a certain rate for each unit
                produced

_____ 20. tying pay to some measure of individual, group, or organizational
                performance

Applications

1. An incentive program initiated at Taco Bell Corporation, that reduced food costs and improved customer service, is referred to as a(n)
   a. employee bonus program.
   b. critical incident program.
   c. forced-choice distribution program.
   d. ranking method program.

2. An incentive plan used at Wood Products Southern Division of Potlach Corporation, which is based upon the completion of a job within a predetermined time, is known as a(n)
   a. piece-rate incentive plan.
   b. employee stock ownership plan.
   c. standard hour plan.
   d. profit-sharing plan.

3. Corporations such as Sears, Combustion Engineering, Borden, and Enhart have adopted the following types of long-term incentive programs, **EXCEPT FOR**
   a. stock price appreciation grants.
   b. restricted stock and restricted cash grants.
   c. performance-based grants.
   d. piecework plans.

4. An example of a highly successful profit-sharing plan implemented at Lincoln Electric, a manufacturer of arc and welding equipment and supplies, is known as a(an)
   a. combined salary and commission plan.
   b. incentive system.
   c. employee assistance program.
   d. standard hour plan.

5. A manufacturer of arc welding equipment and supplies has instituted a highly successful profit sharing plan known as the
   a. combined salary and commission plan.
   b. Lincoln Electric's incentive system.
   c. piece-rate incentive plan.
   d. standard hour plan.

How to Motivate Student Behavior

Motivation can be defined in terms of some outward behavior. Students who are motivated exhibit a greater effort to perform a task than those who are not motivated. Essentially, motivation is the willingness to do something, which is conditioned by the ability to satisfy some need for the student. For instance, the amount of effort a student puts into a class he/she takes determines whether he/she will pass or fail. There are different theories that explain how student behavior is motivated. The expectancy theory proposes that motivation depends on how much a student wants something and how likely he/she thinks that it will be received. If a student perceives that studying and researching will lead to a specific outcome, such as a good grade or a career goal, then he/she is motivated to perform the needed tasks.

Another theory of motivation for student behavior is Maslow's needs hierarchy theory. This theory states that there are five needs ranked in a hierarchical order from lowest to highest. These needs are physiological, safety, belonging, esteem, and self-actualization. A student has to satisfy the lower level needs in order to move up through the hierarchy. A student who is motivated to excel in his/her academics is attempting to satisfy the esteem and self-actualization needs. If the lower level needs are not met, the student will experience difficulty in being motivated to perform well in his/her studies.

SOLUTIONS

Multiple Choice:	True/False:	Matching:
1. b	1. False	1. g
2. c	2. False	2. p
3. a	3. False	3. i
4. c	4. False	4. a
5. d	5. True	5. r
6. b	6. False	6. l
7. c	7. True	7. e
8. d	8. True	8. n
9. a	9. False	9. b
10. a	10. True	10. j
11. b	11. False	11. f
12. d	12. True	12. c
13. b	13. False	13. s
14. a	14. False	14. o
15. d	15. True	15. h
16. b	16. True	16. d
17. c	17. False	17. m
18. a	18. False	18. k
19. b	19. False	19. q
20. d	20. True	20. t
21. d	21. False	
22. b	22. True	
23. a	23. False	
24. d	24. False	
25. a	25. True	

False Statements from True/False

1. Incentive plans **sometimes fail to** satisfy employee needs as well as the organization's needs.
2. The primary purpose of an incentive compensation plan is **measurement and rewards**.
3. One of the **oldest** incentive plans is based on piecework.
4. Straight piecework employees receive a **certain** rate of pay for each unit produced.
6. Piecework is **inappropriate** where quality is more important than quantity.
9. For **employers**, the lump-sum merit program provides financial control by maintaining annual salary expenses to employees.
11. Professional employees can receive compensation beyond base pay in the form of **profit sharing or stock ownership**.
13. Most organizations pay their short-term incentive bonuses in the form of **annual profit plans, payments based on performance rating, and/or achievement of goals**.

14. Balanced scorecards **in terms of executive incentives** are used to measure customer satisfaction, the **ability to innovate**, and product or service leadership.
17. Under the Scanlon Plan, financial incentives based on increases in employee productivity **are offered to all hourly employees**.
18. The Rucker Plan may be used to cover production workers **or expanded to cover all hourly employees.**
19. The financial incentive of the Rucker Plan is based on the historic relationship between the total earnings of **employees** and the production value that **employees** create.
21. Improshare is a bonus plan **not** based on dollar savings **but on productivity gains that result from reducing production time.**
23. The purpose of profit sharing is to **motivate a total commitment** from employees **rather than having them** commit to a specific area of the organization.
24. Employee stock ownership programs (ESOPs) are more likely to serve their intended purposes in **publicly** held companies than in **privately** held ones.

Applications

1. a
2. c
3. d
4. b
5. c

CHAPTER 11

EMPLOYEE BENEFITS

A growing proportion of the compensation employees receive is not provided in the paycheck. Rather, it is paid in the form of benefits that employers increasingly must offer to compete in the labor market or to satisfy union demands or legal requirements. In order to emphasize that these benefits constitute a significant part of the compensation employees are paid; employers increasingly are using the term "total compensation." Different types of employee benefits entail different problems and costs.

LEARNING OBJECTIVES

After studying this chapter you should be able to

 Describe the characteristics of a sound benefits program.

 Indicate management concerns about the costs of employee benefits and discuss ways to control those costs.

 Identify and explain the employee benefits required by law.

 Discuss suggested ways to control the costs of health care programs.

 Describe those benefits that involve payment for time not worked.

 Discuss the recent trends in retirement polices and programs.

 Indicate the major factors involved in the management of pension plans.

 Describe the types of work/life benefits that employers may provide.

CHAPTER SUMMARY RELATING TO LEARNING OBJECTIVES

1 Benefits are an established and integral part of the total compensation package. In order to have a sound benefits program there are certain basic considerations. It is essential that a program be based on specific objectives that are compatible with organizational philosophy and policies as well as affordable. Through committees and surveys a benefit package can be developed to meet employees' needs. Through the use of flexible benefit plans, employees are able to choose those benefits that are best suited for their individual needs. An important factor in how employees view the program is the full communication of benefits information through meetings, printed material, and annual personalized statements of benefits.

2 According to a 2001 study, the costs of employee benefits in that year averaged 37.5 percent of payroll or $16,617 per employee. Since many of the benefits represent a fixed cost, management must pay close attention in assuming more benefit expense. Increasingly, employers are requiring employees to pay part of the costs of certain benefits. Employers also shop for benefit services that are competitively priced.

3 Nearly a quarter of the benefits package that employers provide is legally required. These benefits include employer contributions to Social Security, unemployment insurance, workers' compensation insurance, and state disability insurance. Social Security taxes collected from employers and employees are used to pay three major types of benefits: (1) old-age insurance benefits, (2) disability benefits, and (3) survivors' insurance benefits.

4 The cost of health care programs has become the major concern in the area of employee benefits. Several approaches are used to contain health care costs, including reduction in coverage, increased coordination of benefits, increased deductible or co-payments, use of health maintenance and preferred provider organizations, medical savings accounts, incentives for outpatient surgery and testing, and mandatory second opinions where surgery is indicated. Employee assistance programs and wellness programs may also contribute to cutting the costs of healthcare benefits.

5 Included in the category of benefits that involve payments for time not worked are vacations with pay, paid holidays, sick leave, and severance pay. The typical practice in the United States is to give twenty days' vacation leave and ten holidays. In addition to vacation time, most employees, particularly in white-collar jobs, receive a set number of sick-leave days. A one-time payment of severance pay may be given to employees who are being terminated.

6 Prior to 1979 employers were permitted to determine the age (usually 65) at which their employees would be required to retire. While there is now no ceiling, a growing number of workers choose to retire before age 65. Many employers provide incentives for early retirement in the form of increased pension benefits or cash bonuses. Some organizations provide pre-retirement programs that may include seminars, workshops, and informational materials. The National Council on Aging, the American Association of Retired Persons, and many other organizations are available to assist both employers and employees in preretirement activities.

7 Whether or not to offer a pension plan is the employer's prerogative. However, once a plan is established it is then subject to federal regulation under the Employee Retirement Income Security Act to ensure that benefits will be available when an employee retires. There are two traditional pension plans available – defined benefit and defined contribution. The amount an employee receives upon retirement is based on years of service, average earnings, and age at time of retirement. Pension benefits are typically integrated with social security benefits. Two of the most significant trends are the growth of 401(K) salary reduction plans and cash-balance pension plans. Pension funds may be administered through either a trusteed or an insurance plan. While the Employee Retirement Income Security Act requires that funds be invested where the return will be the greatest, employees often demand a voice in determining where funds will be invested.

8 The types of service benefits that employers typically provide include employee assistance programs, counseling services, educational assistance plans, child care, and elder care. Other benefits are food services, on-site health services, prepaid legal services, financial planning, housing and moving, transportation pooling, purchase assistance, credit unions, social and recreational services, and awards.

REVIEW QUESTIONS

Multiple Choice

Choose the letter of the word or phrase that best completes each statement.

_____ 1. An indirect form of compensation intended to improve the quality of the work lives and the personal lives of employees is the
  a. incentive pay system.
  b. monetary wage.
  c. employee benefit plan.
  d. annual bonus plan.

_____ 2. The communication of employee benefits information improved significantly with passage of the
  a. Equal Pay Act (EPA).
  b. Fair Labor Standards Act.
  c. Right to Privacy Act.
  d. Employee Retirement Income Security Act (ERISA).

objective 1

3. In managing an employee benefits program, management must consider the following **EXCEPT FOR**
   a. union demands.
   b. benefits other employers are offering.
   c. reengineering programs.
   d. tax consequences.

objective 2

4. With a diverse workforce an increasing number of employers are willing to provide benefits to employees who establish
   a. domestic partnership.
   b. health maintenance organizations (HMOs).
   c. human resources plans.
   d. employee vesting.

objective 2

5. The following are standards that enable an employee to qualify under a domestic partnership in an organization, **EXCEPT FOR**
   a. minimum age requirement.
   b. specification of financial independence.
   c. requirement that the couple live together.
   d. requirement that the relationship be a permanent one.

objective 3

6. An act that provides an insurance plan designed to protect covered individuals against loss of earnings resulting from various causes is the
   a. Equal Pay Act.
   b. Social Security Act.
   c. Civil Rights Act.
   d. Employee Retirement Income Security Act.

objective 3

7. Individual employees should not be required to bear the cost of their treatment or loss of income, nor should they be subjected to complicated, delaying, and expensive legal procedures under
   a. workers' compensation insurance.
   b. life insurance.
   c. health insurance.
   d. prescription optical insurance.

objective 3

8. The benefits that receive the most attention from employers today because of high costs and employee concern are
   a. overtime provisions.
   b. prescription optical.
   c. childcare benefits.
   d. health care benefits.

9. Groups that offer routine medical services at a specific site for a fixed fee for each employee visit are called
    a. prescription drug services.
    b. rehabilitation services.
    c. health maintenance organizations.
    d. dental plans.

10. A survey that will tell whether the health maintenance organizations is meeting employee (and employer) expectation needs focuses on the following **EXCEPT FOR**
    a. employee satisfaction with various health maintenance organizations services.
    b. access to health care.
    c. health care competition.
    d. monitoring performance and proficiency of services offered.

11. An important cost containment program that provides employees with comprehensive medical insurance carrying high deductibles is a(n)
    a. medical savings account.
    b. unemployment insurance program.
    c. workers' compensation insurance plan.
    d. Social Security insurance program.

12. A program in which companies commit a specified dollar amount toward health coverage with employees completely free to select their medical help where desired is
    a. unemployment insurance program.
    b. workers' compensation insurance.
    c. Social Security insurance program.
    d. defined-contribution health plan.

13. The category of benefits that includes paid vacations, bonuses given in lieu of paid vacations, payments for holidays not worked, paid sick leave, military and jury duty, and payments for absence due to a death in the family or other personal reasons is called
    a. unemployment insurance.
    b. payment for time not worked.
    c. social security insurance.
    d. payment for time worked.

14. A one-time payment, usually dependent on an individual's years of service, that is given to employees who are being terminated is
    a. unemployment insurance.
    b. supplemental unemployment benefits (SUBs).
    c. vacation pay.
    d. severance pay.

15. Insurance designed to pay for nursing home and other medical costs during old age is known as
    a. long-term care insurance.
    b. prescription optical insurance.
    c. prescription drug insurance.
    d. workers' compensation insurance.

16. An early-retirement incentive in the form of increased pension benefits for several years or a cash bonus is referred to as the
    a. employer buy-out.
    b. silver handshake.
    c. labor contract.
    d. employee sick bank.

17. The type of pension plan where the amount an employee is to receive upon retirement is specifically set forth is
    a. voluntary fringe.
    b. noncontributory holiday.
    c. involuntary benefit.
    d. defined-benefit plan.

18. A tax-deferred plan that allows employees to save through payroll deductions and to have their contributions matched by the employer is known as
    a. supplemental unemployment benefits (SUBs).
    b. unemployment insurance.
    c. 401(k) savings plan.
    d. Social Security insurance.

19. Individuals can file a charge with the Equal Employment Opportunity Commission when they believe that they have been denied benefits because of the following **EXCEPT FOR**
    a. age.
    b. race.
    c. religion.
    d. behavior.

_7_   _____   20. Pension contributions are placed in a trust fund in a
                       a. vesting pension right program.
                       b. trusteed pension plan.
                       c. noncontributory plan.
                       d. undefined contribution plan.

_8_   _____   21. To help workers cope with a wide variety of problems that
                       interfere with job performance, organizations have developed
                       a. employee assistance programs.
                       b. 401(k) plans.
                       c. severance pay packages.
                       d. contributory plans.

_8_   _____   22. A portion of a worker's pay before taxes is set aside for a
                       dependent child with a
                       a. health insurance plans.
                       b. pension programs.
                       c. dependent-care spending account.
                       d. counseling services.

_8_   _____   23. The benefit provided to an older relative by an employee who
                       remains actively at work is called
                       a. elder care.
                       b. dental insurance.
                       c. life insurance.
                       d. health insurance.

_8_   _____   24. To provide a convenience to employees and also to keep them
                       close to the work location, organizations offer
                       a. employee pensions.
                       b. food services.
                       c. legal services.
                       d. 401 (k) plans.

_8_   _____   25. Financial planning programs cover the following **EXCEPT FOR**
                       a. investments.
                       b. tax planning and management.
                       c. estate planning.
                       d. food services.

True/False

Identify the following statements as True or False.

_____ 1. Like any other component of the human resources program, an employee benefits program should be based on specific objectives.

_____ 2. Before a new benefit is introduced, the need for it should first be determined through a consultation with customers.

_____ 3. To accommodate the individual needs of employees, there is a trend toward flexible benefits plans, also known as cafeteria plans.

_____ 4. Since many benefits represent a variable rather than a fixed cost, management must decide whether or not it can afford this cost under less favorable economic conditions.

_____ 5. Organizations that offer benefits to domestic partners are simply extending current benefits, normally full medical and dental plans, to employees.

_____ 6. Legally required employee benefits constitute nearly a quarter of the benefits package that employers provide.

_____ 7. To be eligible for old-age and survivors' insurance as well as for disability and unemployment insurance under the Social Security Act, an individual need not be engaged in employment covered by the act.

_____ 8. Workers' compensation laws typically provide that employees will be paid a disability benefit based on work performance.

_____ 9. A covered employer must grant an eligible employee up to a total of two workweeks of unpaid leave in a two-month period under the Family and Medical Leave Act.

_____ 10. The approaches used to contain the costs of health care benefits include reductions in coverage, increased deductibles or co-payments, and increased coordination of benefits.

_____ 11. Decreasing health care competition, price battles, and high usage rates are all cited causes of lower quality health care.

objective 4

_____ 12. A supplemental pay benefit allows employees to select a doctor of their choice from a list of physicians.

objective 5

_____ 13. Supplemental unemployment benefits plan enables an employee who is working to draw weekly benefits, in addition to state unemployment compensation, from the employer.

objective 5

_____ 14. One of the oldest and most popular employee benefits is group term life insurance, which provides death benefits to beneficiaries and may also provide accidental death and dismemberment benefits.

objective 6

_____ 15. To encourage layoffs, particularly of more recently hired members of protected classes, and to reduce salary and benefit costs, employers often encourage early retirement.

objective 6

_____ 16. Due to the vesting requirements negotiated into most union contracts and more recently required by law, pensions are now based on a reward philosophy.

objective 7

_____ 17. In a contributory plan, contributions are made solely by the employer.

objective 7

_____ 18. Most of the pension plans existing in privately held organizations are noncontributory, whereas those in government are contributory plans.

objective 7

_____ 19. Unlike traditional defined-benefit pension plans, which guarantee payments based on years of service, the 401(k) plans guarantee nothing.

objective 7

_____ 20. An employer can revoke vested pension benefits that have been earned by an employee.

objective 7

_____ 21. Pension funds may be administered through either a trusteed or an insured plan.

objective 8

_____ 22. The increased employment of women with dependent children has created an unprecedented demand for childcare arrangements.

objective 8

_____ 23. Demand for elder care programs will decrease dramatically as baby boomers move into their fifties and find themselves managing organizations.

_____ 24. Although the employer may provide office space and a payroll deduction service, an employee service such as the use of credit unions are operated by the employees under federal and state legislation and supervision.

_____ 25. Many organizations do not offer some type of sports program in which personnel may participate on a voluntary basis.

Matching

Match each term with the proper definition.

Terms

a. contributory plan
b. defined-benefit plan
c. defined-contribution plan
d. elder care
e. employee assistance programs (EAPs)
f. flexible benefits plans (cafeteria plans)
g. health maintenance organizations (HMOs)

h. medical savings plans
i. noncontributory plan
j. preferred provider organization (PPO)
k. silver handshake
l. supplemental unemployment benefits (SUBs)
m. vesting
n. workers' compensation insurance

Definitions

_____ 1. benefit plans that enable individual employees to choose the benefits that are best suited to their particular needs

_____ 2. a guarantee of accrued benefits to participants at retirement age, regardless of their employment status at that time

_____ 3. organizations of physicians and health care professionals that provide a wide range of services to subscribers and dependents on a prepaid basis

_____ 4. care provided to an elderly relative by an employee who remains actively at work

_____ 5. federal- or state-mandated insurance provided to workers to defray the loss of income and cost of treatment due to work-related injuries or illness

_____ 6. a pension plan where contributions are made jointly by employees and employers

_____ 7. a pension plan where contributions are made solely by the employer

_____ 8. services provided by employers to help workers cope with a wide variety of problems that interfere with the way they perform their jobs

_____ 9. a plan that enables an employee who is laid off to draw weekly benefits, in addition to state unemployment compensation, from the employer that are paid from a fund created for this purpose

_____ 10. a pension plan in which the amount an employee is to receive upon retirement is specifically set forth

_____ 11. an early-retirement incentive in the form of increased pension benefits for several years or a cash bonus

_____ 12. a pension plan that establishes the basis on which an employer will contribute to the pension fund

_____ 13. a group of physicians who establish an organization that guarantees lower health care costs to the employer

_____ 14. a high deductible medical insurance plan financed by employer contributions to an employee's individual medical savings account

Applications

_____ 1. Employers that have a diverse workforce, such as Viacon International, Stanford University, Apple Computer, and Microsoft, have begun offering benefits historically reserved for married couples to employees who are over the age of 18 and share living quarters with another adult. Unmarried partners who are responsible for each other's welfare is a
   a. fringe benefit.
   b. domestic partnership.
   c. vesting right.
   d. pension benefit.

_____ 2. Polaroid offers employees an opportunity to try out retirement through an unpaid three-month leave program. They also offer a program that permits employees to gradually cut their hours before retirement. This is an example of a(n)
   a. severance package.
   b. employee pension.
   c. worker compensation program.
   d. pre-retirement program.

7 _____ 3. Enron employees used stock rather than cash to fund their
            a. 401(k) plan.
            b. severance package.
            c. worker buyout.
            d. silver handshake.

8 _____ 4. A program used by the New York Mets and Levi-Strauss to
            provide diagnosis, counseling, and referral for advice or treatment
            for a variety of problems that interfere with the way their
            employees perform their jobs is
            a. severance package.
            b. employee assistance program.
            c. worker buyout.
            d. pre-retirement program.

8 _____ 5. Employee services for parents, offered at Ben & Jerry's Ice
            Cream, include classrooms at the work site that use innovative
            teaching methods for
            a. employee counseling.
            b. elder care.
            c. childcare programs.
            d. legal services.

How to Recognize the Importance of Fringe Benefits

Employee benefits generally refer to various rewards, incentives, and other things of value that an organization provides to its employees beyond their wages, salaries, and other forms of direct financial compensation. Benefits should be more than a laundry list of specific benefit entitlements. They should be a well-developed package of benefits and benefit options that best fulfill the needs of employees and the organization.

There are several types of fringe benefits offered by employers. Laws mandate that all employees must have certain benefits such as social security, unemployment insurance, and worker's compensation. Other benefits include health and dental plans, private pension plans, paid time off in the form of vacation time, holiday pay, sick leave, and personal time. Employers have also included in their benefits package wellness programs, childcare, elder care, and employee assistance programs.
Probably the most important option is health care coverage. While law does not mandate this benefit, it has become standard. With the increasing cost of health care and the rise of managed care, this benefit has been a major concern for employees. The ideal plan is where the employer gives the employee options and pays for a significant portion of the costs.

A popular type of benefit package is a cafeteria-style plan. This often is the best alternative because it allows employees to choose the benefits they really want. Employees are given a list of benefits and costs, and they have the ability to choose any combination that best serves their needs. This is increasingly important with the rise of two-income families. One spouse may have a better health plan with an employer. This plan would allow the other spouse to elect another benefit option and reduce the costs. It also provides flexibility in the benefit selection process. Employees should analyze the benefit options offered by potential employers, and weigh the employment decision accordingly.

SOLUTIONS

Multiple Choice:	True/False:	Matching:
1. c	1. True	1. f
2. d	2. False	2. m
3. c	3. True	3. g
4. a	4. False	4. d
5. b	5. True	5. n
6. b	6. True	6. a
7. a	7. False	7. i
8. d	8. False	8. e
9. c	9. False	9. l
10. c	10. True	10. b
11. a	11. False	11. k
12. d	12. False	12. c
13. b	13. False	13. j
14. d	14. True	14. h
15. a	15. False	
16. b	16. False	
17. d	17. False	
18. c	18. True	
19. d	19. True	
20. b	20. False	
21. a	21. True	
22. c	22 True	
23. a	23. False	
24. b	24. True	
25. d	25. False	

False Statements from True/False

2. Before a new benefit is introduced, the need for it should first be determined through a consultation with **employees**.

4. Since many benefits represent a **fixed** rather than a **variable** cost, management must decide whether or not it can afford this cost under less favorable economic conditions.

7. To be eligible for old-age and survivors' insurance as well as for disability and unemployment insurance under the Social Security Act, an individual **must** be engaged in employment covered by the act.

8. Workers' compensation laws typically provide that employees will be paid a disability benefit based on **percentage of their wages**.

9. A covered employer must grant an eligible employee up to a total of **twelve** workweeks of unpaid leave in a **twelve**-month period under the Family and Medical Leave Act.

11. **Increasing** health care competition, price battles, and high usage rates are all cited causes of lower quality health care.

12. A **preferred provider** organization allows employees to select a doctor of their choice from a list of physicians.

13. Supplemental unemployment benefits plan enables an employee who is **laid off** to draw weekly benefits, in addition to state unemployment compensation, from the employer.

15. To **avoid** layoffs, particularly of more recently hired members of protected classes, and to reduce salary and benefit costs, employers often encourage early retirement.

16. Due to the vesting requirements negotiated into most union contracts and more recently required by law, pensions are now based on **an earnings** philosophy.

17. In a **noncontributory** plan, contributions are made solely by the employer.

20. Vested benefits that have been earned by an employee **cannot** be revoked by an employer.

23. Demand for elder care programs will **increase** dramatically as baby boomers move into their fifties and find themselves managing organizations.

25. Many organizations **do offer** some type of sports program in which personnel may participate on a voluntary basis.

Applications

1. b
2. d
3. a
4. b
5. c

CHAPTER 12

SAFETY AND HEALTH

Safety and health programs have continued to receive employer attention since the passage of the Occupational Safety and Health Act (OSHA). For several reasons discussed in the text, employers have intensified their efforts to create safe work environments. Similarly, they have developed programs to reduce health hazards on the job. Many employees have instituted programs for building better health and for providing assistance to employees. They have developed stress-management programs to teach employees how to minimize the negative effects of job-related stress.

LEARNING OBJECTIVES

After studying this chapter you should be able to

Summarize the general provisions of the Occupational Safety and Health Act (OSHA).

Describe what management can do to create a safe work environment.

Identify the measures that should be taken to control and eliminate health hazards.

Describe the organizational services and programs for building better health.

Explain the role of employee assistance programs in human resources management.

Indicate methods for coping with stress.

CHAPTER SUMMARY RELATING TO LEARNING OBJECTIVES

1 The Occupational Safety and Health Act was designed to assure, so far as possible, safe and healthful working conditions to every working person. In general, the act extends to all employers and employees. The Occupational Safety and Health Act Administration involves setting standards, ensuring employer and employee compliance, and providing safety and health consultation and training where needed. Both employers and employees have certain responsibilities and rights under the Occupational Safety and Health Act. Employers are not only required to provide a hazard-free work environment, but must also keep employees informed about the Occupational Safety and Health Act requirements and must require their employees to use protective equipment when necessary. Under the "right to know" regulation, employers are required to keep employees informed of hazardous substances and instruct them in avoiding the dangers presented. Employees, in turn, are required to comply with the Occupational Safety and Health Act standards, to report hazardous conditions, and to follow all employer safety and health regulations.

2 In order to provide safe working conditions for their employees, employers typically establish a formal program that, in a large percentage of organizations, is under the direction of the human resources manager. The program may have many facets, including providing safety knowledge and motivating employees to use it, making employees aware of the need for safety, and rewarding them for safe behavior. Such incentives as praise, public recognition, and awards are used to involve employees in the safety program. Maintenance of required records from accident investigations provides a basis for information that can be used to create a safer work environment.

3 Job conditions that are dangerous to the health of employees are now receiving much greater attention than in the past. There is special concern for toxic chemicals that proliferate at a rapid rate and may lurk in the body for years without outward symptoms. Concern for health hazards other than those found in industrial processing operations, indoor air pollution, video display terminals, and cumulative trauma disorders, present special problems that must be addressed. Today tobacco smoke is rarely tolerated in the work environment. While there is no evidence that AIDS can be spread through casual contact in the workplace, employers have found that it is important to educate managers and employees about AIDS and to assist those who are afflicted.

4 Along with providing safer and healthier work environments, many employers establish programs that encourage employees to improve their health habits. Some of the larger employers have opened primary care clinics for employees and their dependents to provide better health care service and to reduce costs. Wellness programs that emphasize exercise, nutrition, weight control, and avoidance of harmful substances serve employees at all organizational levels.

5 Virtually all of the larger organizations and many of the smaller ones have found that an employee assistance program is beneficial to all concerned. While emotional problems, personal crises, alcoholism, and drug abuse are often viewed as personal matters, it is apparent that they affect behavior at work and interfere with job performance. An employee assistance program typically provides professional assistance by in-house counselors or outside professionals where needed.

6 An important dimension to health and safety is stress that comes from physical activity and mental or emotional activity. While stress is an integral part of being alive, when it turns into distress it becomes harmful. We have seen that there are many sources of stress that are job-related. In recognizing the need for reducing stress, employers can develop stress-management programs to assist employees in acquiring techniques for coping with stress. In addition, organizations need to take action to redesign and enrich jobs, to clarify the employee's work role, to correct physical factors in the environment, and to take any other actions that will help reduce stress on the job.

REVIEW QUESTIONS

Multiple Choice

Choose the letter of the word or phrase that best completes each statement.

_____   1. The act that has been very effective in reducing the number of
                injuries resulting in lost work time, as well as the number of job-
                related deaths is the
                a. Equal Pay Act.
                b. Age Discrimination and Employment Act.
                c. Occupational Safety and Health Act (OSHA).
                d. Pregnancy Leave Act.

_____   2. One of the responsibilities of the Occupational Safety and Health
                Administration is to develop and enforce
                a. mandatory pregnancy sick days.
                b. mandatory job safety and health standards.
                c. equal pay for equal work.
                d. nondiscriminatory applications pertaining to age requirements.

_____   3. Different types of violations the Occupational Safety and Health
                Administration can cite against an employer include the following
                EXCEPT FOR
                a. discipline procedures.
                b. other-than-serious violations.
                c. serious violations.
                d. willful violations.

4. The government agency that provides a free on-site safety
   consultation service is
   a. Federal Trail Commission.
   b. Occupational Safety and Health Administration.
   c. Food and Drug Administration.
   d. National Labor Relations Board.

5. Once employers are accepted into the Occupational Safety and
   Health Administration's Safety and Health Achievement
   Recognition Program, they may be exempted from
   a. voluntary retirement programs.
   b. employer associations.
   c. affirmative action programs.
   d. programmed inspections for one year.

6. The definition of toxic and hazardous substances, the duties of
   employers and manufacturers to provide health-risk information to
   employees, trade-secret protection, and enforcement provisions
   are statutes addressed under
   a. pregnancy leave.
   b. employee right-to-know laws.
   c. business necessity actions.
   d. bona fide occupational qualifications.

7. The most important role of a safety program is motivating the
   following people in an organization to be aware of safety
   considerations, **EXCEPT FOR**
   a. customers.
   b. managers.
   c. supervisors.
   d. subordinates.

8. Many organizations cover first aid, defensive driving, accident
   prevention techniques, handling of hazardous equipment, and
   emergency procedures in their
   a. affirmative action policy.
   b. safety training programs.
   c. business ethics code.
   d. mission statement.

objective 2   _____   9. Computer training techniques to enhance safety awareness would include the following **EXCEPT FOR**
   a. Internet exercises.
   b. interactive CD-ROMs.
   c. Local Area Networks.
   d. PowerPoint presentations.

objective 2   _____   10. Sealing windows reducing outside air, and "buttoning up" buildings results in
   a. organization culture.
   b. customs and practices.
   c. socialization audit.
   d. sick-building syndrome.

objective 3   _____   11. The most heated workplace health issue in the last decade is
   a. sexual harassment.
   b. pregnancy leave.
   c. business ethics code.
   d. smoking.

objective 3   _____   12. Mini-breaks that involve exercises, properly designed workstations, the changing of positions, and improvement in tool design are ways an organization can prevent
   a. sexual harassment.
   b. chemical hazards.
   c. cumulative trauma disorders.
   d. indoor air quality.

objective 3   _____   13. The "deadly virus" of crime in American work environments is
   a. second-hand smoke.
   b. workplace violence.
   c. job burnout.
   d. video display terminals hazards.

objective 3   _____   14. To minimize the consequences of terrorism, organizations are implementing
   a. emergency evacuation procedure.
   b. labor contracts.
   c. health insurance.
   d. job analysis.

3 _____ 15. Organizations that have employees who conduct initial risk assessment surveys, develop action plans to respond to violent situations, and perform crisis intervention during violent or potentially violent encounters have established
a. crisis management teams.
b. wellness programs.
c. employee right-to-know laws.
d. citation committees.

4 _____ 16. Along with improving working conditions that are hazardous to employee health, many employers provide health services and have programs that encourage employees to improve their
a. alarm reactions.
b. resistance to job burnout.
c. financial status.
d. health habits.

4 _____ 17. Programs that are very popular and produce measurable cost savings, especially when they target high cholesterol, blood pressure counts, high body-fat levels, or smoking, are called
a. mission statements.
b. voluntary protection programs.
c. wellness programs.
d. Material Safety Data Sheets (MSDSs).

5 _____ 18. A program referring employees in need of assistance to in-house counselors or outside professionals is a(n)
a. employee right-to-know program.
b. alarm reaction program.
c. employee assistance program.
d. voluntary protection program (VPP).

5 _____ 19. When managers note that individual productivity is lowered, that morale problems exist, and that absenteeism and substance abuse are increasing, they are identifying the signs of
a. employee satisfaction.
b. employee depression.
c. union busting.
d. external environmental controls.

5 _____ 20. Today one of the major employment issues affecting individuals is
a. drug abuse.
b. recycling of products.
c. global warming.
d. acid rain.

5

_____ 21. Awakening the person to the reality of his or her situation is the first step in helping the
a. individual through cultural shock.
b. wellness committee.
c. union organizing drive.
d. alcoholic.

6

_____ 22. Physical activity and mental or emotional activity are two basic sources of
a. job performance.
b. employee turnover.
c. chronic absenteeism.
d. stress.

6

_____ 23. Positive stress that accompanies achievement and exhilaration is
a. distress.
b. alarm reaction.
c. eustress.
d. job enrichment.

6

_____ 24. High workloads, excessive job pressures, layoffs and organizational restructuring, and global economic conditions are identified as the primary factors in
a. marital success.
b. employee orientation.
c. employee stress.
d. employee training.

6

_____ 25. Inability to voice complaints, poor working conditions, and inadequate recognition can become
a. major stressors.
b. cumulative trauma disorders.
c. sick building syndrome.
d. eustress.

True/False

Identify the following statements as True or False.

1

_____ 1. Improved productivity and wages and the lack of medical expenses coupled with decreased disabilities in the workplace lead to the passage of the Occupational Safety and Health Act in 1970.

2. The Federal Register is the principal source of information on proposed, adopted, amended, and deleted the Occupational Safety and Health Act standards.

3. Typically, the Occupational Safety and Health Act inspectors will arrive at a work site unannounced and ask for a meeting with a representative of the employer.

4. The Occupational Safety and Health Act citations may be issued immediately following inspections or later by mail.

5. Employees are not required to comply with all applicable the Occupational Safety and Health Act standards, to report hazardous conditions, and to follow all employer safety and health rules and regulations, including those prescribing the use of protective equipment.

6. The complaint most registered against the Occupational Safety and Health Administration is the consistently even enforcement efforts by the agency from one political administration to the next.

7. To achieve safe working conditions, the majority of employers have an informal safety program.

8. One of a supervisor's major responsibilities is to communicate to employees the need to work safely.

9. Human resources professionals and safety directors do not encourage employee involvement when designing and implementing safety programs.

10. Penalties for violating safety rules are usually stated in the employee handbook.

11. The supervisor and a member of the safety committee do not need to investigate every accident.

12. The Occupational Safety and Health Act requirements mandate that employers with 11 or more employees maintain records of occupational injuries and illnesses.

13. An injury or illness is a recordable case if it results in death, days away from work, restricted work, transfer to another job, or medical treatment beyond first aid.

14. The Occupational Safety and Health Act is clearly designed to protect the health, as well as the safety, of employees.

15. Hazardous chemical containers do not have to be labeled with the identity of the contents but must state any appropriate hazard warnings.

16. When cumulative trauma disorders result from work activities, these injuries have been held by courts to be compensable injuries entailing workers' compensation payments.

17. It is recognized that better health not only benefits the individual, but also pays off for the organization in reduced absenteeism, increased efficiency, better morale, and other savings.

18. Wellness programs inhibit measurable cost savings to employers and are less effective when organizations target their efforts at specific health risks.

19. The most prevalent problems among employees are personal crises involving marital, family, financial, or legal matters.

20. The National Institute of Mental Health estimates that nearly 17 million Americans suffer from some form of physical impairment every year.

21. In confronting the problem, employers must recognize that alcoholism is a disease that follows a rather unpredictable course.

22. Alcoholism is regarded as a disease, and is always treated as a physical impairment to the employee.

23. Stress becomes distress when a person begins to sense a loss of his feelings of security and adequacy.

24. Career burn out, the least severe stage of distress, generally occurs when a person begins questioning company values.

25. Individual employees in good physical health are immune to stressors in the work environment.

Matching

Match each term with the proper definition.

Terms

a. alarm reaction
b. burnout
c. cumulative trauma disorders
d. depression
e. distress
f. employee right-to-know laws

g. eustress
h. Material Safety Data Sheets (MSDSs)
i. recordable case
j. stress
k. voluntary protection programs (VPPs)

Definitions

_____ 1. injuries involving tendons of the fingers, hands, and arms that become inflamed from repeated stresses and strains

_____ 2. negative emotional state marked by feelings of low spirits, gloominess, sadness, and loss of pleasure in ordinary activities

_____ 3. programs that encourage employers to go beyond the minimum requirements of the Occupational Safety and Health Act

_____ 4. harmful stress characterized by a loss of feelings of security and adequacy

_____ 5. response to stress that basically involves an elevated heart rate, increased respiration, elevated levels of adrenaline in the blood, and increased blood pressure

_____ 6. documents that contain vital information about hazardous substances

_____ 7. positive stress that accompanies achievement and exhilaration

_____ 8. any demand caused by physical, mental, or emotional factors that requires coping behavior

_____ 9. laws that require employers to advise employees of job hazards

_____ 10. most severe stage of distress, manifesting itself in depression, frustration, and loss of productivity

_____ 11. any occupational death, illness, or injury to be recorded in the Occupational Safety and Health Act log (Form 200)

Applications

1. At Stanley Works, Inc., the number one tool for reducing health and safety problems is the company's
   a. Internet.
   b. drug abuse program.
   c. affirmative action program.
   d. voluntary protection program.

2. Employees of Federal Mogel may become "Danger Rangers". These individuals take corrective action after reporting
   a. sexual harassment.
   b. near-miss accidents.
   c. depression.
   d. cumulative trauma disorders.

3. Johnson Controls, Inc., instituted a policy that excluded all women capable of bearing children from its battery factories because they would be exposed of lead. The Supreme Court ruled this was a form of discrimination concerning
   a. social responsibilities.
   b. affirmative action.
   c. ethical codes and rules.
   d. sexual bias.

4. Organizations such as Tenneco, have developed programs that emphasize regular exercise, proper nutrition, weight control, and avoidance of substances harmful to health. These are all examples of
   a. alarm reactions.
   b. employee distress.
   c. wellness programs.
   d. cumulative trauma disorders.

5. A standing plan that has been enacted at Kinko's to ensure a safe, productive work environment and to protect all workers and Kinko's property is an example of
   a. the Occupational Safety and Health Act procedures and guidelines.
   b. drug-free workplace policies.
   c. affirmative action policies.
   d. wellness programs.

How to Inquire about a Safe and Healthy Work Environment

Students are encouraged to inquire about a safe and healthy work environment with perspective employers. Safety is an important concern to everyone, and questions should be generated based on the philosophy of management and their commitment to safety. Students should ask questions related to safety issues, such as what are the major causes of accidents in the workplace? Does the Occupational Safety and Health Act regulate this work environment? Does the employer presently have a safety committee? What is its role and function? Is it a recommending body or does it have functional authority? Does the employer have a logbook to record accidents?

Health related factors are important concerns for employees and should be addressed. Health hazards are those characteristics of the work environment that more slowly and systematically result in damage to the employee's health. Thus, health hazards impair working conditions and can result in decreased productivity and downtime. There are the Occupational Safety and Health Act regulations pertaining to health requirements. Students should address health-related issues, such as exposure to hazardous chemicals or toxic substances. Employers must disclose information to employees concerning any hazard that may pose an injury to their health. A smoking policy is becoming an important issue due to the increased hazard of second hand smoke. For instance, smoking is prohibited in most state and federal offices. There are procedures and rules that may apply and students are encouraged to analyze these regulations.

SOLUTIONS

Multiple Choice:	True/False:	Matching:
1. c	1. False	1. c
2. b	2. True	2. d
3. a	3. True	3. k
4. b	4. True	4. e
5. d	5. False	5. a
6. b	6. False	6. h
7. a	7. False	7. g
8. b	8. True	8. j
9. c	9. False	9. f
10. d	10. True	10. b
11. d	11. False	11. i
12. c	12. True	
13. b	13. True	
14. a	14. True	
15. a	15. False	
16. d	16. True	
17. c	17. True	
18. c	18. False	
19. b	19. True	
20. a	20. False	
21. d	21. False	
22. d	22. False	
23. c	23. True	
24. c	24. False	
25. a	25. False	

False Statements from True/False

1. **Lost** productivity and wages and **increasing** medical expenses coupled with **increased** disabilities in the workplace lead to the passage of the Occupational Safety and Health Act in 1970.
5. Employees **are** required to comply with all applicable the Occupational Safety and Health Act standards, to report hazardous conditions, and to follow all employer safety and health rules and regulations, including those prescribing the use of protective equipment.
6. The complaint most registered against the Occupational Safety and Health Administration is the **uneven** enforcement efforts by the agency from one political administration to the next.
7. To achieve safe working conditions, the majority of employers have a **formal** safety program.

9. Human resources professionals and safety directors **advocate** employee involvement when designing and implementing safety programs.

11. The supervisor and a member of the safety committee **need** to investigate every accident.

15. Hazardous chemical containers **must** be labeled with the identity of the contents **and** must state any appropriate hazard warnings.

18. Wellness programs **produce** measurable cost savings to employers and are **particularly** effective when organizations target their efforts at specific health risks.

20. The National Institute of Mental Health estimates that nearly 17 million Americans suffer from **depression** every year.

21. In confronting the problem, employers must recognize that alcoholism is a disease that follows a rather **predictable** course.

22. Alcoholism is regarded as a disease, **similar to a mental impairment** to the employee.

24. Career burn out, the least severe stage of distress, generally occurs when a person begins questioning **his/her own personal** values.

25. Individuals in good physical health are **better able to cope with** stressors in the work environment.

Applications

1. a
2. b
3. d
4. c
5. b

CHAPTER 13

EMPLOYEE RIGHTS AND DISCIPLINE

The rights of employees to protect their jobs while obtaining fair and just treatment from employers received much attention during the 1990s. On the other side of the balance, are the employer's responsibilities to provide a safe and efficient workplace for employees while expecting productivity and a positive attitude from all jobholders. Issues such as drug testing, smoking on the job, access to one's personnel file, notice of plant closing, and unfair discharge are therefore topics of interest to all organizational members.

When employees exhibit unsatisfactory behavior or performance it may be necessary for an employer to take disciplinary action against them. If the employee is represented by a union, the disciplinary action is likely to be appealed through the grievance procedure provided for in the labor agreement. In a nonunion organization, the aggrieved employee may use an alternative dispute-resolution procedure established specifically by the employer. In either the union or nonunion setting, management may ultimately have to defend its position to a specified individual or group who will decide on the reasonableness of the action taken. To defend themselves successfully, as well as to simply impose fair and objective disciplinary procedures, supervisors and managers need to understand the principles of effective discipline.

Organizational ethics extends beyond the legal requirements of managing employees in human resources management. Managers must comply with governmental regulations to promote an environment free from litigation. However, beyond what is required by law is the question of organizational ethics and the ethical or unethical behavior engaged in by managers.

LEARNING OBJECTIVES

After studying this chapter you should be able to

Explain the concepts of employee rights and employer responsibilities.

Explain the concepts of employment-at-will, wrongful discharge, implied contract, and constructive discharge.

Identify and explain the privacy rights of employees.

 Explain the process of establishing disciplinary policies, including the proper implementation of organizational rules.

 Discuss the meaning of discipline and how to investigate a disciplinary problem.

 Differentiate between the two approaches to disciplinary action.

 Identify the different types of alternative dispute-resolution procedures.

 Discuss the role of ethics in the management of human resources.

CHAPTER SUMMARY RELATING TO LEARNING OBJECTIVES

Employees may claim they have legal rights guaranteeing them fair and equitable treatment while on the job. Employee rights issues frequently involve employer searches, drug testing, or the monitoring of an employee's personal conversation. Employers, however, have the responsibility to provide a safe and secure workplace free from harmful employee acts. When the perceived rights of employees differ with the reasonable responsibilities of management, conflict can result.

Both employees and employers have rights and expectations in the employment relationship. The employment-at-will doctrine regards the rights of employees and employers to terminate the employment relationship while the implied-contract concept is an exception to the employment-at-will doctrine. Under this concept, an employer's oral or written statements may form a contractual obligation that can preclude the automatic termination of employees. Constructive discharge occurs when an employee voluntarily terminates employment but subsequently alleges he or she was forced to quit because intolerable working conditions imposed by the employer. Employees may claim they are retaliated against when employers punish them for exercising their rights under law or for receiving favorable Equal Employment Opportunity Commission or court awards.

Once employed, employees expect certain privacy rights regarding personal freedom from unwarranted intrusion into their personal affairs. These rights extend over such issues as substance abuse and drug testing, searches and surveillance, off-duty privacy rights, e-mail and voice mail privacy, and genetic testing.

4   The human resources department, in combination with other managers, should establish disciplinary policies. This will help achieve both acceptance of policy and its consistent application. To reduce the need for discipline, organizational rules and procedures should be widely known, reviewed on a regular basis, and written and explained to employees. The rules must relate to the safe and efficient operation of the organization. When managers overlook the enforcement of rules, they must reemphasize the rule and its enforcement before disciplining an employee.

5   The term "discipline" has three meanings—punishment, orderly behavior, and the training of employee conduct. When used with employees, discipline should serve to correct undesirable employee behavior, creating within the employee a desire for self-control. This third definition of discipline can only be achieved when managers conduct a complete and unbiased investigation of employee misconduct. The investigation of employee misconduct begins with the proper documentation of wrongdoing. When managers are investigating employee problems they need to know specifically the infraction of the employee, whether the employee knew of the rule violated, and any extenuating circumstances that might justify the employee's conduct. When employees are to receive discipline, the rule must be uniformly enforced and the past work record of the employee must be considered.

6   The two approaches to discipline are progressive discipline and positive discipline. Progressive discipline follows a series of steps based upon increasing the degrees of corrective action. The corrective action applied should match the severity of the employee misconduct. Positive discipline, based upon reminders, is a cooperative discipline approach where employees accept responsibility for the desired employee improvement. The focus is on coping with the unsatisfactory performance and dissatisfactions of employees before the problems become major.

7   Alternative dispute-resolution procedures present ways by which employees exercise their due process rights. The most common forms of alternative dispute-resolutions (ADRs) are step-review systems, peer-review systems, mediation, the open-door system, the ombudsman system, and the use of arbitration.

8   Ethics in human resources management extends beyond the legal requirements of managing employees. Managers engage in ethical behavior when employees are treated in an objective and fair way and when an employee's personal and work-related rights are respected and valued.

REVIEW QUESTIONS

Multiple Choice

Choose the letter of the word or phrase that best completes each statement.

_____ 1. The guarantees of fair treatment that employees expect in protection of their employment status is
   a. employee rights.
   b. equal pay for equal work.
   c. fair employment.
   d. performance appraisal.

_____ 2. The failure to use a reasonable amount of care where such failure results in injury to another person is
   a. punishment.
   b. suspension.
   c. negligence.
   d. severance pay.

_____ 3. When an employee agrees to work for an employer for an unspecified period of time, it creates a relationship of
   a. alternative dispute resolution.
   b. business ethics.
   c. employment-at-will.
   d. negligence.

_____ 4. Oral or written statements made during the pre-employment process or subsequent to hiring are
   a. employment-at-will contracts.
   b. employee rights.
   c. business ethics.
   d. implied contractual rights.

_____ 5. An employee voluntarily terminating his or her employment because of harsh, unreasonable employment conditions placed upon the individual by the employer is
   a. employee assistance.
   b. constructive discharge.
   c. human resources planning.
   d. job evaluation.

_____   6. The matter of personal freedom from unwarranted government or
               business intrusion into personal affairs would be
               a. due process.
               b. job expectancy rights.
               c. rights of privacy.
               d. performance evaluation.

_____   7. The cost to U.S. employers for substance abuse in the workplace
               include the following, **EXCEPT FOR**
               a. fewer mistakes made in the workplace.
               b. safety risks.
               c. more accidents.
               d. benefits costs.

_____   8. Unless state or local laws either restrict or prohibit drug testing,
               private employers have a right to require employees to submit to a
               a. polygraph test.
               b. lie detector test.
               c. psychiatric evaluation.
               d. urinalysis or blood test.

_____   9. It is not uncommon for employers to monitor the behavior of
               individual conduct in the workplace through
               a. job evaluation.
               b. job analysis.
               c. equal pay for equal work.
               d. surveillance techniques.

_____   10. The method used discreetly by employers to discriminate against
               or stigmatize individuals applying for employment or individuals
               currently employed is
               a. merit reviews.
               b. genetic testing.
               c. job security.
               d. disciplinary action.

_____   11. The primary responsibility for preventing or correcting disciplinary
               problems at the workplace rests with an employee's
               a. top-line manager.
               b. labor union.
               c. immediate supervisor.
               d. peers.

12. The foundation for an effective disciplinary system is composed of
    a. organizational rules.
    b. peer reviews.
    c. alternative dispute resolutions.
    d. employment-at-will principle.

13. A progressive form of discipline used when an employee infraction occurs is called the
    a. employee right.
    b. open-door policy.
    c. peer-review system.
    d. hot-stove rule.

14. An essential part of an effective disciplinary system is a(n)
    a. implied contract.
    b. accurate and complete set of work records.
    c. outplacement service.
    d. express contract.

15. To make sure employees are fully aware of the offense and before any disciplinary action is initiated, the supervisor should conduct a(n)
    a. job evaluation.
    b. performance appraisal.
    c. investigative interview.
    d. job analysis.

16. If a thorough investigation shows that an employee has violated an organization rule, the supervisor should impose
    a. due process.
    b. oral warnings.
    c. compensatory damages.
    d. disciplinary action.

17. The two primary approaches to disciplinary action are
    a. progressive and positive discipline.
    b. peer reviews and open door policies.
    c. outplacement and ombudsman services.
    d. employment-at-will and implied contracts.

18. An application of corrective measures by increasing degrees designed to motivate an employee to correct his or her misconduct voluntarily is
    a. constructive discharge.
    b. due process.
    c. progressive discipline.
    d. negative discipline.

19. The approach that focuses on the early correction of misconduct, with the employee taking total responsibility for resolving the problem is
    a. orientation and training.
    b. job security.
    c. positive discipline.
    d. merit reviews.

20. When employees fail to conform to organizational rules and regulations, the final disciplinary action in many cases is a
    a. peer review.
    b. discharge.
    c. verbal warning.
    d. written reprimand.

21. An employee's right to present his or her position during a disciplinary action is
    a. employment-at-will.
    b. due process.
    c. implied contract.
    d. willful discharge.

22. The technique used to describe the different types of employee complaint resolution procedures is
    a. discipline.
    b. employment-at-will principle.
    c. business ethics.
    d. alternative dispute resolution.

23. Listening to an employee's complaint and attempting to resolve it by mediating a solution between the employee and the supervisor is the function of a(n)
    a. shop steward.
    b. corporate executive.
    c. ombudsman.
    d. stockholder.

7   _____ 24. The process that is used primarily to resolve discrimination suits
                        in areas of age, gender, sexual harassment, and race is
                        a. job evaluation.
                        b. arbitration.
                        c. mediation.
                        d. conciliation.

8   _____ 25. The ultimate goal of ethics training is to
                        a. create social responsibility.
                        b. treat employees in a fair and equitable manner.
                        c. implement human resources planning.
                        d. facilitate job enlargement.

True/False

Identify the following statements as True or False.

1   _____ 1. The U.S. Constitution guarantees that jobs are among the specific
                       property rights of employers.

2   _____ 2. The principle of employment-at-will assumes employers are free
                       to terminate the employment relationship at any time, and without
                       notice, for any reason, no reason, or even a bad reason.

2   _____ 3. The significance of wrongful discharge suits is that they challenge
                       the employer's right under the implied employment concept to
                       bilaterally discharge employees.

3   _____ 4. Drug testing is most prevalent among employees in sensitive
                       positions within the public sector, in organizations doing business
                       with the federal government, and in public and private
                       transportation outfits.

3   _____ 5. Employers subject to the Americans with Disabilities Act need not
                       comply with the law's provisions regarding drug addiction.

3   _____ 6. Employees have reasonable expectation of privacy in places
                       where work rules that provide for inspections have been put into
                       effect, they do not have to comply with probable-cause searches
                       by employers.

3   _____ 7. The information kept in an employee's personnel file does not
                       have a significant impact, positive or negative, on career
                       development.

objective 3

_____ 8. The right to privacy does not extend to E-mail and voice mail messages.

objective 4

_____ 9. A major responsibility of the human resources department is to develop and to have top management approve its disciplinary policies and procedures.

objective 4

_____ 10. When taken against employees, disciplinary action should always be thought of as punishment.

objective 5

_____ 11. When preparing documentation, it is important for a manager to record the incident immediately after the infraction takes place, when the memory of it is still fresh, and to ensure that the record is complete and accurate.

objective 5

_____ 12. The investigative interview should concentrate on how the offense violated the performance and behavior standards of the job.

objective 5

_____ 13. An employee's right to representation in a unionized organization does not extend to all interviews with management and organized labor.

objective 6

_____ 14. The sequence and severity of the disciplinary action vary with the type of offense and the circumstances surrounding it.

objective 6

_____ 15. While positive discipline appears similar to progressive discipline, its emphasis is on giving employees reprimands rather than reminders as a way to improve performance.

objective 6

_____ 16. The right of the employee to tell his or her side of the story regarding the alleged infraction of organizational rules is an employee assistance program.

objective 7

_____ 17. A procedure that allows the employee to submit a complaint to successively higher levels of management is the step-review system.

objective 7

_____ 18. The peer-review system can be used as the sole method for resolving employee complaints, or it can be used in conjunction with a step-review system.

objective 7

_____ 19. Two of the major weaknesses of an open-door policy are the willingness of managers to listen honestly to employees and worker willingness to approach managers with their complaints.

_7_ _____ 20. While ombudsmen do not have power to overrule the decision made by an employee's supervisor, they should be able to appeal the decision up the management hierarchy if they believe an employee is not being treated fairly.

_7_ _____ 21. Mediation employs a third-party neutral to assist employees and managers to reach a voluntary agreement unacceptable to both parties.

_7_ _____ 22. Arbitration agreements may prevent employees from suing their employer in court, and may preclude employees from filing discrimination charges with the Equal Employment Opportunity Commission.

_8_ _____ 23. Managers need not comply with governmental regulation to promote an environment free from litigation.

_8_ _____ 24. Compliance with laws and the behavioral treatment of employees are two completely different aspects of the manager's job.

_8_ _____ 25. Many organizations have their own code of ethics that governs relations with employees and the public at large.

Matching

Match each term with the proper definition.

Terms

a. alternative dispute resolution (ADR)
b. constructive discharge
c. discipline
d. due process
e. employee rights
f. employment-at-will principle
g. ethics
h. hot-stove rule

i. mediation
j. negligence
k. ombudsman
l. open-door policy
m. peer-review system
n. positive, or nonpunitive, discipline
o. progressive discipline system
p. step-review system

Definitions

_____ 1. application of corrective measures by increasing stages

_____ 2. system for reviewing employee complaints that utilizes a group composed of equal numbers of employee representatives and management appointees, which functions as a jury since its members weigh evidence, consider arguments, and after deliberation, vote independently to render a final decision

_____ 3. failure to provide reasonable care where such failure results in injury to consumers or other employers

_____ 4. technique applied to different types of employee complaint or dispute-resolution procedures

_____ 5. the use of an impartial neutral to reach a compromise decision in employment disputes

_____ 6. employee's right to present his or her position during a disciplinary action

_____ 7. system of discipline that focuses on the early correction of employee misconduct, with the employee taking total responsibility for correcting the problem

_____ 8. policy of settling grievances that identifies various levels of management above the immediate supervisor for employee contact

_____ 9. the right of an employer to fire an employee without giving a reason and the right of an employee to quit when he or she chooses

_____10. system for reviewing employee complaints and disputes by successively higher levels of management

_____11. definitions include (1) treatment that punishes; (2) orderly behavior in an organizational setting; or (3) training that molds and strengthens desirable conduct or corrects undesirable conduct and develops self-control

_____12. designated individual from whom employees may seek counsel for the resolution of their complaints

_____13. guarantees of fair treatment from employers, particularly regarding an employee's right to privacy

_____ 14. the progressive form of discipline that gives warning, is effective immediately, is enforced consistently, and applies to all employees in an impersonal and unbiased way

_____ 15. set of standards of conduct and moral judgments that help to determine right and wrong behavior

_____ 16. an employee voluntarily terminating his or her employment because of harsh, unreasonable employment conditions placed upon the individual by the employer

Applications

2 _____ 1. In a leading U.S. Supreme Court case, *Toussaint v Blue Cross and Blue Shield of Michigan*, the court found that an employee handbook was enforceable under the concept of
   a. due process.
   b. implied contract.
   c. alternative dispute resolution.
   d. express contract.

3 _____ 2. General Electric employs tiny fish-eye lenses installed behind pinholes in walls and ceilings to observe employees suspected of crimes. This is known as a(n)
   a. surveillance technique.
   b. open-door policy.
   c. alternative dispute resolution.
   d. hot-stove rule.

5 _____ 3. A management tool that Goodyear Aerospace and Arizona State University uses to correct, mold, and perfect knowledge, attitude, behavior, and conduct is known as
   a. business ethics.
   b. commercial codes.
   c. alternative dispute resolution.
   d. discipline.

7 _____ 4. Turner Brothers and Polaroid resolve employee complaints through a system of justice called the
   a. hot-stove rule.
   b. disciplinary procedure.
   c. peer-review system.
   d. arbitration process.

7 _____ 5. In an attempt to resolve employee conflict in the workplace,
                companies such as Rockwell, Johnson and Johnson, and Volvo
                have utilized a(n)
                a. ombudsman.
                b. hearing officer.
                c. arbitration panel.
                d. consulting firm.

How to Develop and Use Ethical Codes in the Business World

Ethical codes are extremely relevant especially when working an organization that is customer driven. For example, at IBM, their mission is to be customer-driven to create consumer satisfaction at all costs. In joining an organization, the student must have orientation and training on ethical codes, policies, and procedures.

Ethics can be defined as a set of standards of acceptable conduct and moral judgment. Ethics provides cultural guidelines, organizational or societal, that help decide between proper or improper conduct. Ethics in human resources management extends beyond the legal requirements of managing employees. Managers engage in ethical behavior when employees are treated in an objective and fair way and when an employee's personal and work-related rights are respected and valued.

Organizations have ethics committees to provide training to employees. The ultimate goal of ethics training is to avoid ethical behavior and adverse publicity; to gain a strategic advantage; but most of all, to treat employees in a fair and equitable manner, recognizing them as productive members of the organization.

SOLUTIONS

Multiple Choice:	**True/False:**	**Matching:**
1. a	1. False	1. o
2. c	2. True	2. m
3. c	3. False	3. j
4. d	4. True	4. a
5. b	5. False	5. i
6. c	6. False	6. d
7. a	7. False	7. n
8. d	8. True	8. l
9. d	9. True	9. f
10. b	10. False	10. p
11. c	11. True	11. c
12. a	12. True	12. k
13. d	13. True	13. e
14. b	14. True	14. h
15. c	15. False	15. g
16. d	16. False	16. b
17. a	17. True	
18. c	18. True	
19. c	19. False	
20. b	20. True	
21. b	21. False	
22. d	22. False	
23. c	23. False	
24. b	24. True	
25. b	25. True	

False Statements from True/False

1.   The U.S. Constitution **carries no mandate that** guarantees that jobs are among the specific property rights of employers.
3.   The significance of wrongful discharge suits is that they challenge the employer's right under the **employment-at-will** concept to bilaterally discharge employees.
5.   Employers subject to the Americans with Disabilities Act **must** comply with the law's provisions regarding drug addiction.
6.   Employees have **no** reasonable expectation of privacy in places where work rules that provide for inspections have been put into effect; they **must** comply with probable-cause searches by employers.
7.   The information kept in an employee's personnel file **can have** a significant impact, positive or negative, on career development.

10. When taken against employees, disciplinary action should **never** be thought of as punishment.
15. While positive discipline appears similar to progressive discipline, its emphasis is on giving employees **reminders** rather than **reprimands** as a way to improve performance.
16. The right of the employee to tell his or her side of the story regarding the alleged infraction of organizational rules is **due process**.
19. Two of the major weaknesses of an open-door policy are the **unwillingness** of managers to listen honestly to employees and worker **reluctance** to approach managers with their complaints.
21. Mediation employs a third-party neutral to assist employees and managers to reach a voluntary agreement **acceptable** to both parties.
22. Arbitration agreements may prevent employees from suing their employer in court; **they cannot** preclude employees from filing discrimination charges with the Equal Employment Opportunity Commission.
23. Managers **must comply** with governmental regulation to promote an environment free from litigation.

Applications

1. b
2. a
3. d
4. c
5. a

CHAPTER 14

THE DYNAMICS OF LABOR RELATIONS

Workers unionize so they can influence employer decisions affecting their employment conditions and general welfare. When employees are unionized, Human Resources policies can no longer be determined unilaterally by the employer. Instead, these policies and practices are subject to the terms of the labor agreement that has been negotiated with the union. A major responsibility of the local union officers is to ensure that these terms are observed and that the rights of members provided by the agreement are protected. Labor agreements, which determine conditions of employment for union members, are achieved through collective bargaining. Bargaining success depends not only on the skills of the negotiators, but also on the power each side can exercise to support its bargaining demands. Once the contract is ratified, its terms and conditions of employment bind both parties until it is once again renegotiated. During the period the contract is in force, the parties learn to cooperate through the administration of the agreement. When conflict arises over the rights the contract grants to each side, the grievance/arbitration provisions of the contract are invoked to resolve these differences.

LEARNING OBJECTIVES

After studying this chapter you should be able to

 Identify and explain the principle federal laws that provide the framework for labor relations.

 Explain the reasons employees join unions.

 Describe the process by which unions organize employees and gain recognition as their bargaining agent.

 Discuss the bargaining process and the bargaining goals and strategies of a union and an employer.

Differentiate the forms of bargaining power that a union and an employer may utilize to enforce their bargaining demands.

 Describe a typical union grievance procedure and explain the basis for arbitration awards.

 Discuss some of the contemporary challenges to labor organizations.

CHAPTER SUMMARY RELATING TO LEARNING OBJECTIVES

1 The Railway Labor Act (1926) affords collective bargaining rights to workers employed in the railway and airline industries. The Norris-LaGuardia Act (1932) imposes limitations on the granting of injunctions in labor-management disputes. Most private employees are granted representation rights through the Wagner Act (1935), which has helped to protect and encourage union organizing and bargaining activities. The passage of the Taft-Hartley Act (1947) and the Landrum-Griffin Act (1959) has served to establish certain controls over the internal affairs of unions and their relations with employers.

2 Studies show that workers unionize for different economic, psychological, and social reasons. While some employees may join unions because they are required to do so, most belong to unions because they are convinced that unions help them to improve their wages, benefits, and various working conditions. Employee unionization is largely caused by dissatisfaction with managerial practices and procedures.

3 A formal union organizing campaign will be used to solicit employee support for the union. Once employees demonstrate their desire to unionize through signing authorization cards, the union will petition the National Labor Relations Board (NLRB) for a secret-ballot election. If 51 percent of those voting in the election vote for the union, the NLRB will certify the union as the bargaining representative for all employees in the bargaining unit.

Negotiating a labor agreement is a detailed process. Each side will prepare a list of proposals it wishes to achieve while additionally trying to anticipate those proposals desired by the other side. Bargaining teams must be selected and all proposals must be analyzed to determine their impact on and cost to the organization. Both employer and union negotiators will be sensitive to current bargaining patterns within the industry, general cost-of-living trends, and geographical wage differentials. Managers will establish goals that seek to retain control over operations and to minimize costs. Union negotiators will focus their demands around improved wages, hours, and working conditions. An agreement will be reached when both sides compromise their original positions and final terms fall within the limits of the parties' bargaining zone. Traditionally, collective bargaining between labor and management has been adversarial. Presently, there is an increased interest in nonadversarial negotiations – negotiations based on mutual gains and a heightened respect between the parties. FMCS interest-based bargaining (IBB) is one form on nonadversarial negotiations.

The collective bargaining process includes not only the actual negotiations but also the power tactics used to support negotiating demands. When negotiations become deadlocked, bargaining becomes a power struggle to force from either side the concessions needed to break the deadlock. The union's power in collective bargaining comes from its ability to picket, strike, or boycott the employer. The employer's power during negotiations comes from its ability to lock out employees or to operate during a strike by using managerial or replacement employees.

When differences arise between labor and management, they will normally be resolved through the grievance procedure. Grievance procedures are negotiated and thus reflect the needs and desires of the parties. The typical grievance procedure will consist of three, four, or five steps, each step having specific filing and reply times. Higher-level managers and union officials will become involved in disputes at the higher steps of the grievance procedure. The final step of the grievance procedure may be arbitration. Arbitrators will render a final decision to problems not resolved at lower grievance steps.

The submission agreement is a statement of the issue to be solved through arbitration. It is simply the problem the parties wish to have settled. The arbitrator must answer the issue by basing the arbitration award on four factors: the contents of the labor agreement, (or employment policy), the submission agreement as written, testimony and evidence obtained at the hearing, and various arbitration standards developed over time to assist in the resolution of different types of labor-management disputes. Arbitration is not an exact science since arbitrators will give varying degrees of importance to the evidence and criteria by which disputes are resolved.

REVIEW QUESTIONS

Multiple Choice

Choose the letter of the word or phrase that best completes each statement.

1. The act that severely restricted the ability of employers to obtain an injunction forbidding a union from engaging in peaceful picketing, boycotts, or various striking activities is the
   a. Taft-Hartley Act.
   b. Wagner Act.
   c. Norris-LaGuardia Act.
   d. Landrum-Griffin Act.

2. The agency responsible for administering and enforcing the Wagner Act is the
   a. Affirmative Action Committee.
   b. Equal Employment Opportunity Commission.
   c. Occupational Safety and Health Administration.
   d. National Labor Relations Board.

3. Union self-organizing activities and collective bargaining were legalized through the
   a. Wagner Act.
   b. Taft-Hartley Act.
   c. Norris-LaGuardia Act.
   d. Landrum-Griffin Act.

4. The Landrum-Griffin Act of 1959, states that every union member has been given the following rights, **EXCEPT FOR**
   a. nominating candidates for union office.
   b. voting in union election or referendums.
   c. attending union meetings.
   d. creation of featherbedding.

5. The strongest reasons to join a labor union are the traditional issues of dissatisfaction with wages, benefits, and
   a. management prerogatives.
   b. working conditions.
   c. compulsory arbitration.
   d. job design.

2 _____ 6. When employees perceive that managerial practices regarding promotion, transfer, shift assignment, or other job-related policies are administered in an unfair or biased manner, they may seek
a. decertification.
b. mediation.
c. unionization.
d. binding arbitration.

2 _____ 7. The major concerns for which employees join unions involve
a. social needs and status.
b. esteem and self-actualization.
c. job enlargement and enrichment.
d. achievement and physiological requirements.

3 _____ 8. Unions have been shocked into more aggressive and creative tactics in organizing strategies to counteract employer anti-union campaigns and to compensate for a(n)
a. closed-shop agreement.
b. decline in membership.
c. organizational picketing.
d. wildcat strike.

3 _____ 9. Once the union is certified, the employer is obligated to begin negotiations leading toward a(n)
a. grievance.
b. wildcat strike.
c. authorization card.
d. labor agreement.

3 _____ 10. Unions seek greater participation in management decisions that involve such issues as subcontracting of work, productivity standards, and job content as a result of
a. job security.
b. management prerogatives.
c. working conditions.
d. hours of work.

3 _____ 11. A chief advantage of belonging to the AFL-CIO is the provision that affords protection against
a. duel unionism.
b. authorization cards.
c. raiding by other unions.
d. primary boycotts.

3 _____ 12. Public-sector legislation affecting human resource management includes the following **EXCEPT FOR**
a. Executive Orders
b. Civil Service Reform Act of 1978.
c. state laws.
d. Equal Pay Act.

4 _____ 13. In collective bargaining there are economic pressures in the form of lockouts, plant closures, and the replacement of strikers that are used by the
a. business agent.
b. labor union.
c. employer.
d. shop steward.

4 _____ 14. In collective bargaining, all matters concerning rates of pay, wages, hours of employment, or other conditions of employment are examples of
a. mandatory subjects.
b. voluntary issues.
c. illegal subjects.
d. unauthorized subjects.

4 _____ 15. Areas or subjects where management and labor are free to bargain, but neither side can force the other side to bargain over such topics are
a. mandatory subjects.
b. involuntary issues.
c. illegal subjects.
d. permissive issues.

4 _____ 16. Illegal subjects in collective bargaining would include the closed shop security agreement and
a. wages and salaries.
b. compulsory dues check-off.
c. working conditions.
d. hours of work.

4 _____ 17. The area within which the union and the employer are willing to concede when negotiating is called the
a. bargaining zone.
b. impasse zone.
c. management lockout.
d. wildcat strike.

_4_ _____ 18. The refusal of a group of employees to perform their jobs and withhold their services when negotiations become deadlocked is a
a. lockout.
b. primary boycott.
c. strike.
d. grievance procedure.

_5_ _____ 19. When a union asks its members or customers not to patronize a business where there is a labor dispute, it is asking for a
a. labor strike.
b. company lockout.
c. slowdown.
d. primary boycott.

_5_ _____ 20. A third party that can be utilized to recommend a compromise when the disputing parties are unable to resolve a deadlock is called a(n)
a. mediator.
b. negotiator.
c. business agent.
d. narrator.

_5_ _____ 21. An individual that has binding authority to resolve disputes arising in connection with the administration of an agreement is a(n)
a. mediator.
b. arbitrator.
c. business agent.
d. human resource director.

_5_ _____ 22. In the public sector, where strikes are largely prohibited, a common method used in the attempt to resolve bargaining deadlocks is
a. conciliation.
b. interest arbitration.
c. outsourcing.
d. performance appraisal.

_6_ _____ 23. Considered by some authorities to be the heart of the bargaining agreement, the safety valve that gives flexibility to the whole system of collective bargaining is the
a. arbitration panel.
b. primary boycott.
c. grievance procedure.
d. closed shop security provision.

24. Unions have a legal obligation to provide assistance to members who are pursuing a grievance under the
    a   secondary boycott award.
    b. employment-at-will doctrine.
    c. closed shop security provision.
    d. fair representation doctrine.

25. Arbitrators use the following factors when deciding cases, **EXCEPT FOR**
    a. written content of the labor agreement.
    b. submission agreements presented to the arbitrator.
    c. testimony and evidence offered during the hearing.
    d. mediation cases that will influence the mediator's award.

True/False

Identify the following statements as True or False.

1. The primary purpose of the Railway Labor Act is to create the use of injunctions between labor and management.

2. Before an injunction may be issued, employers need not show that lack of an injunction will cause greater harm to the employer than to the union.

3. The Wagner Act created the National Labor Relations Board to govern labor relations in the United States.

4. Because of the high incidence of strikes after World War II, the Taft-Hartley Act created the Federal Mediation and Conciliation Service to help resolve negotiating disputes.

5. Most labor-organizing campaigns are undertaken by union organizers rather than employees.

6. At least 30 percent of the employees must sign authorization cards before the National Labor Relations Board will hold a representation election.

7. Employers may not initiate legal action should union members and/or their leaders engage in any unfair labor practices during the organizing effort.

8. The petition to hold representation elections is always initiated by the employer.

9. Unlike the AFL-CIO, national unions hold conventions to pass resolutions, amend their constitutions, and elect officers.

10. Depending on the size of the local union, one or more officers, in addition to the business representative, may be paid by the union to serve on a full-time basis.

11. Union stewards are normally elected by union members within their department and are always paid a salary.

12. In the local union, officers, by federal law, must run for reelection at least every third year.

13. Most state legislatures have granted public employees the right to strike.

14. Negotiators for an employer should develop a written plan called a proposal, which includes the collective bargaining strategy.

15. The negotiation of a labor agreement can have some of the characteristics of a poker game, with each side attempting to determine its opponent's position while not revealing its own.

16. Once bargaining begins, an employer is not obligated to negotiate in good faith with the union's representative over conditions of employment.

17. When negotiations become deadlocked, the employer's bargaining power largely rests on being able to continue operations in the face of a strike or to shut down operations entirely.

18. If employees decide to strike the organization, employers have the right to hire replacement workers.

19. A mediator assumes the role of a decision-maker and determines what the settlement between the two parties should be.

20. If a grievance cannot be resolved through the grievance procedure, each disputing party must decide whether to use arbitration to resolve the case.

_____ 21. A grievance should be viewed as something to be won or lost from the perspective of the government.

_____ 22. The arbitration hearing process begins with the swearing-in of witnesses and the introduction of the submission agreement, which is a statement of the problem to be resolved.

_____ 23. The arbitration award should include not only the arbitrator's decision but also the rationale for it.

_____ 24. Arbitrators are essentially constrained to decide cases on the basis of the wording of the labor agreement but never to the facts, testimony, and evidence presented at the hearing.

_____ 25. Targeted prospects for union growth include low wage service workers on the bottom tier of the U.S. economy and recent immigrants who are working.

Matching

Match each term with the proper definition.

Terms

a. arbitrator
b. authorization card
c. bargaining power
d. bargaining unit
e. bargaining zone
f. business unionism
g. collective bargaining process
h. craft unions
i. employee associations
j. exclusive representation

k. fair-representation doctrine
l. grievance procedure
m. industrial union
n. interest-based bargaining
o. labor relations process
p. rights arbitration
q. unfair labor practices (ULPs)
r. union shop
s. union steward

Definitions

_____ 1. specific employer and union illegal practices that operate to deny employees their rights and benefits under federal labor law

_____ 2. unions that represent skilled craft workers

_____ 3. a statement signed by an employee authorizing a union to act as a representative of the employee for purposes of collective bargaining

_____ 4. employee who as a nonpaid union official represents the interests of members in their relations with management

_____ 5. logical sequence of four events: (1) workers desire collective representation, (2) union begins its organizing campaign, (3) collective negotiations lead to a contract, and (4) the contract is administered

_____ 6. term applied to the goals of U.S. labor organizations, which collectively bargain for improvements in wages, hours, job security, and working conditions

_____ 7. labor organizations that represent various groups of professional and white-collar employees in labor-management relations

_____ 8. provision of the labor agreement that requires employees to join the union as a requirement for their employment

_____ 9. unions that represent all workers--skilled, semiskilled, unskilled--employed along industry lines

_____ 10. group of two or more employees who share common employment interests and conditions and may reasonably be grouped together for purposes of collective bargaining

_____ 11. formal procedure that provides for the union to represent members and nonmembers in processing a grievance

_____ 12. doctrine under which unions have a legal obligation to provide assistance to both members and nonmembers in labor relations matters

_____ 13. arbitration over interpretation of the meaning of contract terms or employee work grievances

_____ 14. process of negotiating a labor agreement, including the use of economic pressures by both parties

_____ 15. third-party neutral who resolves a labor dispute by issuing a final decision in the disagreement

_____ 16. problem-solving bargaining based on a win-win philosophy and the development of a positive long-term relationship

_____ 17. the power of labor and management to achieve their goals through economic, social, or political influence

_____18. the legal right and responsibility of the union to represent all bargaining unit members equally regardless of whether employees join the union or not

_____19. area within which the union and the employer are willing to concede when bargaining

Applications

_____1. The United Auto Workers are aggressively organizing workers at auto plants in southern states. This is an example of unions that are actively organizing
a. unionized personnel.
b. first line management.
c. supervisors.
d. unrepresented employees.

_____2. In an organizing effort by the United Auto Workers at a Nissan plant, the union lost the election because workers were satisfied with the
a. grievance procedure.
b. business agent.
c. participatory style of management.
d. union steward.

_____3. In *NLRB v Town and Country Electric, Inc.*, the U.S. Supreme Court held that employers cannot discriminate hiring or other terms of employment against
a. union salts.
b. shop stewards.
c. business agents.
d. national staff representatives.

_____4. A Teamster truck driver refusing to deliver produce to a food store whose employees are picketing with the United Food & Commercial Workers Union is an example of a
a. strike.
b. wildcat strike.
c. lockout.
d. primary boycott.

(7 _____   5. Foreign subsidiaries of American corporations such as Nike,
Westinghouse, and Xerox have been accused by labor unions of
a. primary boycotts.
b. exporting American jobs.
c. wildcat strikes.
d. grievance procedures.

How to Create and Manage a Non-union Operation

The primary objective of managing a non-union operation is paramount for the success
of an organization. Management must create an environment that is built upon
openness, trust, and respect for their employees. They must demonstrate a clear
appreciation of their employees and permit them to experience a high degree of job
satisfaction. A management style that challenges employees and establishes high
expectations to their commitment of work is essential. Creating the right type of culture
that is closely knit among management and their employees is recommended.
Employee empowerment is a reality to permit decision making to take place closest to
the point of action where it has to be made. To keep a union out employee needs must
be identified and met. Management must offer extrinsic and intrinsic rewards to their
employees. Extrinsic rewards include money, bonus, and other financial incentives.
Intrinsic rewards include recognition, self-esteem, and self-actualizing experiences.
The ultimate goal is for employees to be challenged and develop to their fullest
potential. These recommendations will assist management in maintaining and
achieving a union free environment.

SOLUTIONS

Multiple Choice:	True/False:	Matching:
1. c	1. False	1. q
2. d	2. False	2. h
3. a	3. True	3. b
4. d	4. True	4. s
5. b	5. False	5. o
6. c	6. True	6. f
7. a	7. False	7. i
8. b	8. False	8. r
9. d	9. False	9. m
10. b	10. True	10. d
11. c	11. False	11. l
12. d	12. True	12. k
13. c	13. False	13. p
14. a	14. True	14. g
15. d	15. True	15. a
16. b	16. False	16. n
17. a	17. True	17. c
18. c	18. True	18. j
19. d	19. False	19. e
20. a	20. True	
21. b	21. False	
22. b	22. True	
23. c	23. True	
24. d	24. False	
25. d	25. True	

False Statements from True/False

1. The primary purpose of the Railway Labor Act is to **avoid service interruptions resulting from disputes between railroads and their operating unions**.
2. Before an injunction may be issued, employers **must** show that lack of an injunction will cause greater harm to the employer than to the union.
5. Most labor-organizing campaigns are undertaken by **employees rather than union organizers**.
7. Employers **may** initiate legal action should union members and/or their leaders engage in any unfair labor practices during the organizing effort.
8. The petition to hold representation elections is **usually** initiated by the **union**.
9. **Similar to** the AFL-CIO, national unions hold conventions to pass resolutions, amend their constitutions, and elect officers.
11. Union stewards are normally elected by union members within their department and **serve without union pay**.
13. Most state legislatures **have not** granted public employees the right to strike.

16. Once bargaining begins, an employer **is obligated** to negotiate in good faith with the union's representative over conditions of employment.
19. A **arbitrator** assumes the role of a decision-maker and determines what the settlement between the two parties should be.
21. A grievance **should not** be viewed as something to be won or lost from the perspective of the government.
24. Arbitrators are essentially constrained to decide cases on the basis of the wording of the labor agreement **including** the facts, testimony, and evidence presented at the hearing.

Applications

1. d
2. c
3. a
4. a
5. b

CHAPTER 15

INTERNATIONAL HUMAN RESOURCES MANAGEMENT

A large percentage of the corporations in the United States are engaged in international business. Many of them are multinational corporations (MNCs) and thus have extensive facilities and human resources in foreign countries. The management of MNCs poses special problems. The cultural environment in which MNCs operate is especially important, and managers must be selected carefully and then trained to be effective in a specific environment. Differences that one finds among countries in the performance of HRM functions are reviewed briefly as a background for further study.

LEARNING OBJECTIVES

After studying this chapter you should be able to

 Identify the types of organizational forms used for competing internationally.

 Explain how domestic and international HRM differ.

 Discuss the staffing process for individuals working internationally.

 Identify the unique training needs for international assignees.

 Reconcile the difficulties of home-country and host-country performance appraisals.

 Identify the characteristics of a good international compensation plan.

 Explain the major differences between U.S. and European labor relations.

CHAPTER SUMMARY RELATING TO LEARNING OBJECTIVES

1 There are four basic ways to organize for global competition: (1) The international corporation is essentially a domestic firm that has leveraged its existing capabilities to penetrate overseas markets; (2) the multinational corporation has fully autonomous units operating in multiple countries in order to address local issues; (3) the global corporation has a world view but controls all international operations from its home office; and (4) the transnational corporation uses a network structure to balance global and local concerns.

2 International HRM places greater emphasis on a number of responsibilities and functions such as relocation, orientation, and translation services to help employees adapt to a new and different environment outside their own country.

3 Because of the special demands made on managers in international assignments, many factors must be considered in their selection and development. Though hiring host-country nationals or third-country nationals automatically avoids many potential problems, expatriate managers are preferable in some circumstances. The selection of the latter requires careful evaluation of the personal characteristics of the candidate and his or her spouse.

4 Once an individual is selected, an intensive training and development program is essential to qualify that person for the assignment. Wherever possible, development should extend beyond information and orientation training to include sensitivity training and field experiences that will enable the manager to understand cultural differences better. Those in charge of the international program should provide the help needed to protect managers from career development risks, reentry problems, and culture shock.

5 Although home-country managers frequently have formal responsibility for individuals on foreign assignment, they may not be able to fully understand expatriate experiences because geographical distances pose severe communication problems. Host-country managers may be in the best position to observe day-to-day performance but may be biased by cultural factors and may not have a view of the organization as a whole. To balance the pros and cons of home-country and host-country evaluations, performance evaluations should combine the two sources of appraisal information.

6 Compensation systems should support the overall strategic intent of the organization but be customized for local conditions. For expatriates, in particular, compensation plans must provide an incentive to leave the United States; enable maintenance of an equivalent standard of living; facilitate repatriation; provide for the education of children; and make it possible to maintain relationships with family, friends, and business associates.

In many European countries, Germany, for example, employee representation is established by law. Organizations typically negotiate the agreement with the union at a national level, frequently with government intervention. Since European unions have been in existence longer than their U.S. counterparts, they have more legitimacy and much more political power. In Europe, it is more likely for salaried employees and managers to be unionized.

REVIEW QUESTIONS

Multiple Choice

Choose the letter of the word or phrase that best completes each statement.

_____   1. A multinational firm that maintains control of operations back in
                the home office can be viewed as a
                a. domestic corporation.
                b. global corporation.
                c. polycentric organization.
                d. geocentric organization.

_____   2. The type of organization that attempts to achieve the local
                responsiveness of a multinational corporation while also achieving
                the efficiencies of a global firm is a(n)
                a. domestic business.
                b. global business.
                c. transnational corporation.
                d. international organization.

_____   3. Communications, religion, values and ideologies, education, and
                social structure of a country are examples of a(n)
                a. cultural environment.
                b. economic environment.
                c. employee and customer rights.
                d. physical environment.

_____   4. The country in which an international business operates is the
                a. third world country.
                b. domestic country.
                c. home country.
                d. host country.

5. International HRM differs from domestic HRM in respect to placing greater emphasis on the following **EXCEPT FOR**
   a. relocation.
   b. orientation.
   c. job analysis programs.
   d. translation.

6. The following are different sources of employees with whom to staff international operations **EXCEPT FOR**
   a. preferential union shops.
   b. home-country nationals.
   c. host-country nationals.
   d. third-country nationals.

7. Natives of the host country who manage international operations are known as
   a. expatriate managers.
   b. third-country nationals.
   c. global managers.
   d. host-country nationals.

8. In recruiting and selecting, a multinational organization assigns individuals from their domestic operations. These people are known as
   a. host-country nationals.
   b. home-country nationals.
   c. third-country nationals.
   d. underdeveloped country nationals.

9. Compared to the United States, employee recruitment in other countries is subject to
   a. management rights.
   b. management prerogatives.
   c. more government regulation.
   d. marketing myopia practices.

10. A document issued by a government granting authority to a foreign individual to seek employment in that government's country is a
   a. work permit.
   b. debit card.
   c. trade agreement.
   d. green card.

_3_ _____ 11. Foreign workers invited to come to a country to perform needed labor are usually referred to as
  a. human resource specialists.
  b. operative employees.
  c. guest workers.
  d. immigrants.

_3_ _____ 12. The most prevalent reasons for failure among expatriates working in foreign countries are
  a. technical limitations.
  b. family and lifestyle issues.
  c. economic issues.
  d. religious beliefs.

_3_ _____ 13. The assembly of people of multiple nationalities who can work together effectively on projects that span multiple countries is a
  a. trade agreement.
  b. domestic work group.
  c. cartel arrangement.
  d. transnational team.

_3_ _____ 14. The following are methods of selection most commonly used by corporations operating internationally **EXCEPT FOR**
  a. assessment centers.
  b. interviews.
  c. tests.
  d. labor contracts.

_4_ _____ 15. A manager equipped to run an international business is a(n)
  a. global manager.
  b. operating supervisor of a local firm.
  c. operating employee.
  d. ethnocentric employee.

_4_ _____ 16. Most executives agree that the biggest problem for the foreign business traveler is
  a. exchange rate conversion.
  b. communicating in different languages.
  c. strategic planning.
  d. accepting bribes.

17. Managerial attitudes and behaviors are influenced by the society in which managers have
    a. job evaluation.
    b. received their education and training.
    c. performance appraisals.
    d. job analysis backgrounds.

18. Studying cultural differences can be helpful to managers in identifying and understanding cultural
    a. augmented skills and the balance-sheet approach.
    b. core skills and guest workers.
    c. work attitudes and motivation.
    d. work permits and work certificates.

19. A disorientation that causes perpetual stress experienced by people who settle overseas for extended periods is
    a. culture shock.
    b. culture environment.
    c. foreign exchange.
    d. social culture disease.

20. One of the principal causes of failure among employees working internationally is
    a. socialization privacy.
    b. expatriate malfeasance.
    c. political upheaval.
    d. lack of training.

21. Although the home-country and host-county superiors may tell an expatriate how well he or she is doing, it is also important for expatriates to provide feedback on the following **EXCEPT FOR**
    a. the support received.
    b. the obstacles they face.
    c. suggestions about the assignment.
    d. polographic material.

22. To be effective, an international compensation program must include the following **EXCEPT FOR**
    a. providing an incentive to leave the home country.
    b. facilitating reentry to the home country.
    c. providing education for local host-nationals.
    d. maintaining family, friends, and business associates.

_____ 23. A compensation system designed to match the purchasing power in a person's home country is a
a. job analysis program.
b. balance-sheet approach to management.
c. job description.
d. job specification.

_____ 24. The role of unions varies from country to country and depends on the following factors **EXCEPT FOR**
a. mobility between labor and management.
b. level of Gross Domestic Product.
c. homogeneity of labor.
d. level of employment.

_____ 25. A higher form of worker participation in management where decision-making is shared between labor and the management is known as
a. codetermination.
b. joint venturing.
c. legitimate power.
d. self-managed teams.

True/False

Identify the following statements as True or False.

_____ 1. The international corporation is essentially a domestic firm that builds on its existing capabilities to penetrate home markets.

_____ 2. To balance a "global/local" dilemma, a transnational corporation uses a network structure that coordinates specialized facilities positioned around the world.

_____ 3. The internationalization of U.S. corporations has grown at a faster pace than the internationalization of human resource management.

_____ 4. All large corporations have a part-time staff of human resource specialists devoted to assisting in the globalization process.

_____ 5. Third-country nationals are natives of a country other than the home country or the host country.

6. Recently there has been a trend to use only expatriates in the lower management positions.

7. Employee recruitment in the United States is subject to more government regulation than in other countries.

8. The employment of non-nationals throughout the globe may involve lower direct labor costs.

9. In the United States, managers tend to emphasize seniority, with the most-senior person getting the job.

10. One of the toughest jobs facing many organizations is finding employees who can meet the demands of working in a foreign environment.

11. Core skills are considered critical to an employee's success abroad.

12. Failure rate is the percentage of impatriates who perform unsatisfactorily on the job they are charged to perform.

13. The success rate of male expatriates has been estimated to be far superior to that of women.

14. The methods of selection most commonly used by corporations operating internationally are interviews, assessment centers, and tests.

15. Because foreign language fluency is important in all aspects of international business, a large percentage of Americans are skilled in a language other than English.

16. In large part, managerial attitudes and behaviors are influenced by the cultural society in which managers have received their education and training.

17. An important dimension of leadership, international or domestic, is the degree to which managers invite employee participation in decision-making.

18. Repatriation is the process of employee transition back home from an international assignment.

19. All companies have career development programs designed for repatriating employees.

_5_ _____ 20. Individuals frequently accept international assignments because they know they can acquire skills and experiences that will make them more valuable to their companies.

_5_ _____ 21. One big advantage of using host-country evaluations is that local cultures may influence one's perception of how well an individual is performing.

_6_ _____ 22. Labor costs are one of the biggest motivators for an organization's international expansion.

_6_ _____ 23. Host-country employees are generally paid on the basis of productivity, time spent on the job, or a combination of these factors.

_6_ _____ 24. Expatriate compensation programs rest on the cash-flow approach, a system designed to equalize the purchasing power of employees at comparable positions living overseas and in the home country.

_7_ _____ 25. The collective bargaining process can vary widely among countries, especially with regard to the role that government plays.

Matching

Match each term with the proper definition.

Terms

a. augmented skills
b. balance-sheet approach
c. codetermination
d. core skills
e. cultural environment
f. culture shock
g. expatriates, home-country nationals
h. failure rate
i. global corporation
j. global manager

k. guest workers
l. host country
m. host-country nationals
n. international corporation
o. multinational corporation (MNC)
p. repatriation
q. third-country nationals
r. transnational corporation
s. transnational teams
t. work permit/work certificate

Definitions

_____ 1. foreign workers invited into a foreign labor market to perform needed labor

_____ 2. perceptual stress experienced by people who settle overseas

_____ 3. firm with independent business units operating in multiple countries

_____ 4. skills helpful in facilitating the efforts of expatriate managers

_____ 5. natives of the host country

_____ 6. representation of labor on the board of directors of a company

_____ 7. firm that has integrated worldwide operations through a centralized home office

_____ 8. compensation system designed to match the purchasing power of a person's home country

_____ 9. government document granting a foreign individual the right to seek employment

_____ 10. country in which an international corporation operates

_____ 11. employees from the home country who are sent on international assignment

_____ 12. communication, religion, values and ideologies, education, and social structure of a country

_____ 13. domestic firm that uses its existing capabilities to move into overseas markets

_____ 14. teams composed of members of multiple nationalities working on projects that span multiple countries

_____ 15. skills considered critical in an employee's success abroad

_____ 16. firm that attempts to balance local responsiveness and global scale via a network of specialized operating units

_____ 17. manager equipped to run an international business

_____ 18. percentage of expatriates who do not perform satisfactorily

_____19. natives of a country other than the home country or the host country

_____20. process that helps employees make the transition back home after a foreign assignment

Applications

_____ 1. Japanese companies such as Matsushita and NEC tend to treat the world market as a unified whole and try to combine activities in each country to maximize efficiency on a
   a. balance-sheet analysis.
   b. global scale.
   c. host-country national.
   d. local basis.

_____ 2. British Airways has a team of Human Resources directors who travel around the world to update host-country managers on international concerns and
   a. policies and programs.
   b. work permits and work certificates.
   c. foreign exchange and balance-sheet analysis.
   d. domestic and third-country trade laws.

_____ 3. To help employees think through the pros and cons of international assignments, companies such as EDS and Deloitte & Touche give them
   a. HRM ethics programs.
   b. social responsibility programs.
   c. job specification programs.
   d. self-selection instruments.

_____ 4. A program designed by Monsanto to prepare employees for reverse culture shock, the disorientation a person feels in trying to adjust to life at home, is known as
   a. expatriation.
   b. codetermination.
   c. repatriation.
   d. augmented skills.

_____ 5. At Renault, the French government-owned automobile manufacturer, unions make use of political pressures in their bargaining with managers, who are essentially
   a. government employees.
   b. operative employees.
   c. management consultants.
   d. mediators.

How to Prepare for an International Assignment for a Multinational Corporation

In the recruiting and selection process for an international assignment, students should understand the preparation required for this opportunity. This would include an understanding of the host nation's culture, political and legal framework, and customs that may prevail in the foreign national's country. Once selected, students should undertake an intensive training and development program. Development should extend beyond information and orientation training to include sensitivity training and field experiences that will enable the student to better understand cultural differences. Students should seek the support of the person(s) in charge of the international program in order to avoid career development risks, reentry problems, and culture shock.

The socialization process of the foreign national's culture and customs is an important orientation objective. To understand fully the challenges of the international assignment, students should be able to adapt to the methodology of the foreign country's business practices. Finally, students should not impose American values and business practices in the foreign country. Preparation includes understanding the customs and practices that exist in the foreign national's culture.

SOLUTIONS

Multiple Choice:	True/False:	Matching:
1. b	1. False	1. k
2. c	2. True	2. f
3. a	3. True	3. o
4. d	4. False	4. a
5. c	5. True	5. m
6. a	6. False	6. c
7. d	7. False	7. i
8. b	8. True	8. b
9. c	9. False	9. t
10. a	10. True	10. l
11. c	11. True	11. g
12. b	12. False	12. e
13. d	13. False	13. n
14. d	14. True	14. s
15. a	15. False	15. d
16. b	16. True	16. r
17. b	17. True	17. j
18. c	18. True	18. h
19. a	19. False	19. q
20. d	20. True	20. p
21. d	21. False	
22. c	22. True	
23. b	23. True	
24. b	24. False	
25. a	25. True	

False Statements from True/False

1. The international corporation is essentially a domestic firm that builds on its existing capabilities to penetrate **overseas** markets.
4. **Most** large corporations have a **full-time** staff of human resource **managers** devoted to assisting in the globalization process.
6. Recently there has been a trend to use only expatriates in the **top** management positions.
7. Employee recruitment in the United States is subject to **less** government regulation than in other countries.
9. In the United States, managers tend to emphasize seniority, with the **best-qualified** person getting the job.
12. Failure rate is the percentage of **expatriates** who perform unsatisfactorily on the job they are charged to perform.
13. The success rate of **female** expatriates has been estimated to be far superior to that of **men**.

15. Foreign language fluency is important in all aspects of international business, **however** a **small** percentage of Americans are skilled in a language other than English.

19. **Unfortunately, not all** companies have career development programs designed for repatriating employees.

21. One **problem** of using host-country evaluations is that local cultures may influence one's perception of how well an individual is performing.

24. Expatriate compensation programs rest on the **balance-sheet** approach, a system designed to equalize the purchasing power of employees at comparable positions living overseas and in the home country.

Applications

1. b
2. a
3. d
4. c
5. a

CHAPTER 16

CREATING HIGH-PERFORMANCE WORK SYSTEMS

The relevance of high-performance work systems is integral for HR practices that amplify employee knowledge, skill, commitment, and flexibility. The system begins with implementing empowered work teams to perform key business processes. Training of team members is paramount, and reward systems are used to motivate behavior. When each subsystem compliments one another, the end result is an internal and external fit to create a holistic system. For the system to function effectively, it must have top management support as well as the labor union. The objective or end result is the high-performance work system benefiting both the employees and the organization.

LEARNING OBJECTIVES

After studying this chapter you should be able to

 Discuss the underlying principles of high-performance work systems.

 Identify the components that make up a high-performance work system.

 Describe how the components fit together and support strategy.

 Recommend processes for implementing high-performance work systems.

 Discuss the outcomes for both employees and the organization.

 Explain how the principles of high-performance work systems apply to small and medium-sized, as well as large, organizations.

CHAPTER SUMMARY RELATING TO LEARNING OBJECTIVES

1 High-performance work systems are specific combinations of HR practices, work structures, and processes that maximize employee knowledge, skill, commitment, and flexibility. They are based on contemporary principles of high-involvement organizations. These principles include shared information, knowledge development, performance-reward linkages, and egalitarianism.

2 High-performance work systems are composed of several interrelated components. Typically, the system begins with designing empowered work teams to carry out key business processes. Team members are selected and trained in technical, problem-solving, and interpersonal skills. Reward systems often have group and organizational incentives, though skill-based pay is regularly used to increase flexibility and salaried pay plans are used to enhance an egalitarian environment. Leadership tends to be shared among team members, and information technology is used to make sure that employees have the information they need to make timely and productive decisions.

3 The pieces of the system are only important in terms of how they help the entire system function. When all the pieces support and complement one another, high-performance work systems achieve internal fit. When the system is aligned with the competitive priorities of the organization as a whole, it achieves external fit as well.

4 Implementing high-performance work systems represents a multidimensional change initiative. High-performance work systems are much more likely to go smoothly if a business case is first made. Top-management support is critical, and so too is the support of union representatives and other important constituents. HR representatives are often helpful in establishing a transition structure to help the implementation progress through its various stages. Once the system is in place, it should be evaluated in terms of its processes, outcomes, and ongoing fit with strategic objectives of the organization.

5 When implemented effectively, high-performance work systems benefit both the employees and the organization. Employees have more involvement in the organization, experience growth and satisfaction, and become more valuable as contributors. The organization also benefits from high productivity, quality, flexibility, and customer satisfaction. These features together can provide an organization with a sustainable competitive advantage.

6 The principles of HPWS apply in small and medium-sized organization work settings as well as in large organizations. Progressive organizations of all sizes have successfully implemented high performance work systems.

REVIEW QUESTIONS

Multiple Choice

Choose the letter of the word or phrase that best completes each statement.

1. The specific combination of human resource practices, work structures, and processes that maximize employee knowledge, skill, commitment, and flexibility is known as
   a. high-performance work systems.
   b. labor-intensive organizations.
   c. self-managed teams.
   d. external integration.

2. One of the primary principles that support high-performance work systems is
   a. job turnover linkage.
   b. complacency evolution.
   c. sharing information.
   d. employment transfer linkage.

3. The principle that includes selecting the best and the brightest candidates available in the labor market and providing all employees opportunities to continuously hone their talents is
   a. shared information.
   b. egalitarianism.
   c. knowledge development.
   d. external fit.

4. When employees pursue outcomes that are mutually beneficial to themselves and the organization, this process is known as the
   a. job knowledge linkage.
   b. performance-reward linkage.
   c. principle of egalitarianism.
   d. concept of shared information.

5. The concept that eliminates status and power differences and, in the process, increases collaboration and teamwork is
   a. shared information.
   b. performance-reward linkage.
   c. knowledge development.
   d. egalitarianism.

6. Moving power downward in organizations by empowering employees frequently requires
   a. structural changes.
   b. bureaucratic changes.
   c. centralized instruction.
   d. cross-training.

7. Emphasis on teamwork, involvement, and continuous improvement requires that employees develop a broader understanding of work processes performed by others around them rather than rely on just knowing their own jobs through
   a. cooperate downsizing.
   b. internal fit.
   c. cross-training.
   d. external fit.

8. In order to link pay and performance, high-performance work systems often include some type of
   a. glass ceiling.
   b. employee incentives.
   c. process audit.
   d. external fit.

9. By paying employees on the basis of the number of different job skills they have, high-performance work systems may also incorporate
   a. piece-rate plans.
   b. standard-hour plans.
   c. performance evaluation.
   d. skill-based pay plans.

10. In addition to linking pay and performance, high-performance work systems are also based on the principle of
   a. egalitarianism.
   b. process auditing.
   c. cross-functional training.
   d. internal fit.

11. Managers and supervisors in high-performance work systems have the following roles **EXCEPT FOR**
   a. coaches.
   b. facilitators.
   c. authoritarian leaders.
   d. integrators of team efforts.

12. An addition to the framework of high-performance work systems, vital to business performance is
    a. centralized management organizations.
    b. rigid organization structures.
    c. authoritarian leadership.
    d. communication and information technologies.

13. High-performance work systems cannot succeed without accurate and timely information, which includes the following **EXCEPT FOR**
    a. business plans and goals.
    b. deprivation of core competencies.
    c. unit and corporate operating results.
    d. competitor performance.

14. The condition that exists when all internal elements of the work system complement and reinforce each other is
    a. job enlargement.
    b. external fit.
    c. job analysis.
    d. internal fit.

15. A strategy that begins with an analysis and discussion of competitive challenges, organizational value, and the concerns of employees and results in a statement of the strategies being pursued by the organization is known as a
    a. external fit.
    b. process audit.
    c. internal fit.
    d. job evaluation.

16. A model that helps managers assess the strategic alignment of their work systems is the
    a. HR Scorecard.
    b. Theory X Model.
    c. Theory Y Model.
    d. Maslow Model.

17. To get initial commitment to high-performance work systems, managers have to build a case that the changes are needed for the
    a. internal fit.
    b. external fit.
    c. success of the organization.
    d. efficiency of the closed system.

18. Autocratic styles of management and confrontational approaches to labor negotiations are being challenged by more enlightened approaches that promote
    a. adventurous and technological programs.
    b. coercion and communication.
    c. cooperation and collaboration.
    d. conflict and coordination.

19. In order to establish an alliance, managers and labor representatives should try to create a(n)
    a. adversarial system.
    b. "win-win" situation.
    c. balance-sheet approach.
    d. "win-lose" approach.

20. Most labor-management alliances are made legitimate through some tangible symbol of a(n)
    a. informal commitment.
    b. culture icon.
    c. trade agreement.
    d. formal commitment.

21. An effective means of ensuring that democracy and fairness prevail, which also keeps the parties focused is
    a. coercion.
    b. conflict.
    c. command performance.
    d. procedure.

22. One of the mistakes that organizations can make in implementing high-performance work systems is
    a. effective communication.
    b. allocating too few resources to the effort.
    c. cooperation and trust.
    d. recognition and respect.

23. The evaluation process that focuses on whether the high-performance work system has been implemented as designed is
    a. internal fit.
    b. performance appraisal.
    c. process audit.
    d. external fit.

4 _____   24. The advantage of high-performance work systems is that they are
   a. flexible and adaptable.
   b. autocratic and coercive.
   c. divisive in conflict.
   d. manipulative and confrontational.

5 _____   25. The following are organizational outcomes that result from using high-performance work systems **EXCEPT FOR**
   a. lower productivity.
   b. lower costs.
   c. better responsiveness to customers.
   d. higher profitability.

True/False

Identify the following statements as True or False.

1 _____   1. Without timely and accurate information about the business, employees can do little more than simply carry out orders and perform their roles in a relatively perfunctory way.

1 _____   2. When employees are given timely information about business performance, plans, and strategies, they are more likely to make good suggestions for improving the business and to cooperate in major organizational changes.

1 _____   3. Employees in high-performance work systems need to learn "real time," on the job, using traditional approaches to solve novel problems.

1 _____   4. A time-tested adage of management is that the interests of employees and organizations naturally diverge.

1 _____   5. Productivity can improve when introducing egalitarianism by having people who once worked in opposition begin to work together.

2 _____   6. High-performance work systems combine various work structures, human resource practices, and management processes to maximize employee performance and well-being.

2 _____   7. Total quality management and reengineering have driven many organizations to redesign their workflow by focusing on the key business processes that drive voluntary layoffs.

objective 2   _____   8. Work redesign, in and of itself, does not constitute a high-performance work system.

objective 2   _____   9. Recruitment tends to be both broad and intensive in order to create the best pool of job candidates.

objective 2   _____   10. Training is focused on ensuring that employees have the skills needed to assume greater responsibility in a high-performance work environment.

objective 2   _____   11. Because high-performance work systems ask many different things from employees, it is easy to isolate one single compensation approach that works for everyone.

objective 2   _____   12. The open-pay plan is yet another way to create a more egalitarian environment that discourages employee involvement and commitment.

objective 2   _____   13. In a growing number of organizations, leadership is shared among team members.

objective 2   _____   14. The richest form of communication occurs face to face between sender and receiver.

objective 2   _____   15. High-performance work systems can succeed without timely and accurate communications.

objective 3   _____   16. External fit occurs when all the internal elements of the work system complement and reinforce one another.

objective 3   _____   17. A situation in which the high-performance work system supports the organization's goals and strategies is known as internal fit.

objective 4   _____   18. One of the best ways to communicate the business needs is to show employees the business' current performance and capabilities.

objective 4   _____   19. Two-way communication can result in better decisions, and it may help to diminish the fears and concerns of employees.

objective 4   _____   20. Building commitment to high-performance work systems is a one-time activity.

4 _____ 21. The bottom-up approach communicates manage support and clarity, while the top-down approach ensures employee acceptance and commitment.

5 _____ 22. A potential benefit to employees from high-performance work systems is they are likely to be more satisfied and find that their needs for growth are more fully met.

5 _____ 23. Implementing high-performance work systems is an easy task, even though systems are complex, and they require a good deal of close partnering among executives, line managers, HR professionals, union representatives, and employees.

5 _____ 24. Because high-performance work systems are simple to implement, organizations that are successful are simple to copy.

6 _____ 25. The philosophies, principles, and techniques that underlie high-performance work systems are equally appropriate to the management of small and medium-sized organizations.

Matching

Match each term with the proper definition.

Terms

a. cross-training
b. high-performance work system (HPWS)
c. internal fit
d. process audit
e. external fit

Definitions

_____ 1. situation in which all the internal elements of the work system complement and reinforce one another

_____ 2. situation in which the work system supports the organization's goals and strategies

_____ 3. specific combination of HR practices, work structures, and processes that maximizes employee knowledge, skill, commitment, and flexibility

_____ 4. determining whether the high-performance work system has been implemented as designed

_____ 5. training of employees in job areas closely related to their own

Applications

1 _____ 1. Edward Lawler and his associates at the Center for Effective
             Organization at the University of Southern California have worked
             with Fortune 1000 corporations to identify the primary principles
             that support
             a. highly centralized organizations.
             b. low-performance work systems.
             c. autocratic leadership styles.
             d. high-performance work systems.

2 _____ 2. Federal Express and Colgate-Palmolive have been able to
             establish a work environment that facilitates teamwork by
             a. redesigning the work flow.
             b. creating responsibility gaps.
             c. expanding organizational structures.
             d. centralizing authority.

3 _____ 3. Xerox uses a planning process known as "Managing for Results,"
             which begins with a statement of
             a. leadership of the firm.
             b. cooperate downsizing.
             c. corporate values and priorities.
             d. responsibility gaps.

4 _____ 4. Solectron Corporation, winner of the Baldrige National Quality
             Award, tried to implement a high-performance work system to
             capitalize on the knowledge and experience of its employees by
             incorporating
             a. authoritarian leaders.
             b. self-managed teams.
             c. responsibility gaps.
             d. politics in the firm.

5 _____ 5. Organizations such as Wal-Mart, Microsoft, and Southwest
             Airlines have been able to enjoy a competitive advantage by
             a. integrating business and employee concerns.
             b. developing an autocratic style.
             c. creating authoritative management.
             d. implementing coercive and confrontational tactics.

How To Apply High-Performance Work Systems To Small, Medium, And Large Scale Organizations

High-performance work systems (HPWS) have become a recent trend for organizations in order to become more efficient and profitable. HPWS can be defined as a specific combination of human resource practices, work structures, and processes that maximize employee knowledge, skill, commitment, and flexibility. The principles of HPWS apply in small and medium-sized organizational work settings as well as in large organizations. For example, progressive organizations of all sizes have successfully implemented team-based work systems, adopted staffing practices that select high-quality employees, developed training programs that continually update employee skills, and utilized compensation practices that support specific organizational goals. The important element is that these organizations have accomplished these tasks in a coordinated and integrative manner. In smaller organizations, a system approach to organizational design is adopted to combine human resource practices, work structures, and processes that effectively utilize employee competencies. In these small businesses, the human resource function is the responsibility of line management. The line manager must recruit and select among a pool of talent, orient and train these individuals, and assume many of the human resource functions. As the organization grows, the staff function of human resource management becomes a reality for the human resource department who accepts the responsibilities that have been developed in this course.

Regardless of the organization's size, evidence suggests that the use of high-performance work systems has led to increased profitability. Research has shown that human resource practices are aggressive activities that create a stronger competitive advantage relative to other firms. Today, the human resource plan is an integrative approach in developing a holistic system with other departments of the small, medium, and large-size organizations. An objective is to recruit and select the most qualified individuals to perform the necessary tasks to achieve organizational goals.

SOLUTIONS

Multiple Choice:	**True/False:**	**Matching:**

Multiple Choice:

1. a
2. c
3. c
4. b
5. d
6. a
7. c
8. b
9. d
10. a
11. c
12. d
13. b
14. d
15. a
16. a
17. c
18. c
19. b
20. d
21. d
22. b
23. c
24. a
25. a

True/False:

1. True
2. True
3. False
4. True
5. True
6. True
7. False
8. True
9. True
10. True
11. False
12. False
13. True
14. True
15. False
16. False
17. False
18. True
19. True
20. False
21. False
22. True
23. False
24. False
25. True

Matching:

1. c
2. e
3. b
4. d
5. a

False Statements from True/False

3. Employees in high-performance work systems need to learn "real time," on the job, using **innovative new** approaches to solve novel problems.
7. Total quality management and reengineering have driven many organizations to redesign their workflow by focusing on the key business processes that drive **customer value**.
11. Because high-performance work systems ask many different things from employees, it is **difficult** to isolate one single compensation approach that works for everyone.
12. The open-pay plan is yet another way to create a more egalitarian environment that **encourages** employee involvement and commitment.
15. High-performance work systems **cannot** succeed without timely and accurate communications.
16. **Internal** fit occurs when all the internal elements of the work system complement and reinforce one another.

17. A situation in which the high-performance work system supports the organization's goals and strategies is known as **external** fit.
20. Building commitment to high-performance work systems is **an ongoing** activity.
21. The **top-down** approach communicates manage support and clarity, while the **bottom-up** approach ensures employee acceptance and commitment.
23. Implementing high-performance work systems is **a difficult** task, systems are complex, and they require a good deal of close partnering among executives, line managers, HR professionals, union representatives, and employees.
24. Because high-performance work systems are **difficult** to implement, organizations that are successful are **difficult** to copy.

Applications

1. d
2. a
3. c
4. b
5. a